I hope ;

Dave McGowan

A TICKET TO THE DANCE
A Civil War soldier's trip to Hell and back

By: David L. McGowan

ISBN: 1-4196-9159-7
ISBN-13: 9781419691591

Visit www.booksurge.com to order additional copies.

DEDICATION

This writing is dedicated to all those men and women who have served in the armed forces of the United States of America during times of war. It is to those individuals we hold dearest to our hearts for protecting our freedoms and allowing us to pursue our individual dreams without oppression.

It is especially dedicated to my one and only brother, Spec 4 William Lewis McGowan who was killed May 14, 1969 at the battle of Hamburger Hill in Vietnam.

- David L. McGowan

PRELUDE

The origins of the American Civil War were surrounded with the complex issues of slavery, federalism, party politics, expansionism, and modernization during the ante-bellum period.

As the North and the South developed its own individual societies, two separate regional identities emerged. The North's economic system was based on free labor, family farms, industry, commerce, and transportation with a rapidly growing European urban population. The South's economic system was based on slave labor on a settled plantation system. Their population growth was through high birth rates and expansionism in the southwest. The South had few cities or towns and little manufacturing. However, they produced 90 percent of the world's cotton and through that one single economic factor the southern states were able to control the national government for many years.

In the 1850s, America's boundaries were expanding. Northern Abolitionists denounced slavery as a social evil and claimed all new states should be slave free and in order to force the end to slavery they wanted to add a tax on cotton producers. The South controlled the Federal government and was able to pass the Kansas-Nebraska Act, allowing each new state to declare by election if they were to be free or slave and that law was upheld by the Supreme Court during Buchanan's Presidency. This so outraged the Northern Abolitionists that it caused the creation of a new political party, the "Republicans" in 1858.

In 1860, the new Republican Party split the vote between the Whigs and the Democrats and won the Presidency. This fear of possible economic losses so outraged the plantation owners who were the politicians of that time that preparations were started immediately to secede. Two-thirds of the White southern population owned no slaves, but politicians used the tactics of declaring that the states' rights would be lost to a federally controlled system under Lincoln and their heritage would be gone forever. Thus began four years of hardship and the loss of an entire generation of young men.

TABLE OF CONTENTS

CHAPTER 1
James Boyden

I have lived my entire 19 years on this earth within
the confinement of the mountains of Cattaraugus County,
New York. Even though their beauty was breathtaking,
I always felt as though I was being trapped inside the
tall walls of green, unable to see the sights outside this
valley. Many times I've wondered to myself what kind of
civilization may lie over the hills that were protected by
these luscious green Appalachian Mountains. Stories about
the great cities that lie along the east coast of America
and the vast flat lands of the new territories to the west
were often told. Each time I would hear of such places like
New York City or Baltimore I would feel an ache in my
stomach signaling to me go and experience these places
for myself.

My parents came here from Vermont with many
other families who took advantage of being able to buy
cheap farmland from the Holland Land Company. We
lived on a 65-acre farm outside the village of Ellington.
Don't get me wrong, it's not that I am ungrateful for my

surroundings; I have grown very fond of fishing from the cool clear water of the Conewango Creek and hunting the abundance of wild game in these mountains—it's just that I have an itch inside me that refuses to go away; an overwhelming desire to see for myself the wonders of our country and to experience what it is like to walk the streets of some of these great cities. The winters here are very cold and the snow comes in abundance and stays until the late spring days of April. The winter winds are harsh on the skin and during the last three winters, we could sometimes go a good month without seeing another soul—other than our own family.

I have three older brothers and one older sister who have since removed themselves from the farm and have taken on their own adventure in farming not very far away. That leaves me here to help Pa along with my other siblings: Lucy and Joseph, both younger than I. When the war broke out last spring, I had wanted to volunteer right away. Everyone in our valley had said the war would be over in a few months, so the window of opportunity for me to volunteer was short. But luck was against me then, as things were really hard at home. Pa is getting on in years and was feeling pretty poorly from a broken leg he had received during the winter. That bad leg prevented him from doing the spring planting, so I had to stay and fill in for him. I couldn't leave the farm, no matter how much I'd wanted to go along with my friends. But now, some six months later, things were different, Pa's leg has healed, Joseph can do more as he is only two years younger than me, and the war has faltered—the President has asked for another 100,000 men. This time I'm determined not to miss the opportunity; this time I mean to leave here and have at my adventure.

The word had spread far and wide that Colonel Thomas Parker would be in the Village of Randolph on August 17, 1861 giving a recruitment speech. I was determined to be there and hear what he had to say. It was a warm morning, but the skies were clear when I hitched up one of our three horses to a buggy and left for Randolph just after breakfast. Pa knew where I was off to. We had spoken quite a bit of my thoughts about doing my duty as a citizen last spring. It was then he said to me, "This war is about squashing a rebellion of the rich plantation owners who want to make their own government since they can't take over ours." Pa wasn't the most intelligent person on this Earth, but he had common sense and he could always tell when someone was less than honest when they spoke. He was a large, tall man, who only shaved once a week when he bathed. His face was rugged, his hands were like leather, and his frame was square and strong by sight. He was never one for small talk as he thought it was a waste of energy. He simply said to me, "Get back before supper or your Ma will worry."

It was a long ride, about five miles and the sun was beating pretty hot as I approached the village, I could see a large mass of people who had congregated at the point where Main Street meets the Jamestown Road. There was a mixed crowd of men from all ages and a few women, but the number must have been upwards of 100. I quickly tied up the horse and walked over to listen to what people were saying. I stood beside a man named Frank Jones, who I recognized as having worked in the Dry Goods Store.

"Where did all these people come from?" I asked him.

"They are from everywhere, Bowen, East Randolph, Sinclairville, Carr Corners, Cold Spring, Napoli, Conewango, Steamburgh, Silver Creek, even Onoville. Some have been here since last evening."

There was a band from East Randolph playing patriotic music and just as we began to speak again the band stopped playing and a man stood up on a cracker box and introduced himself as Major Brooks. He was a small, slender man wearing a smart-looking uniform and hat. He spoke in a loud articulate manner and was speaking more like a motivated hellfire and brimstone preacher than a speechmaker. His stories of recent events against the Flag of our country had everybody, including myself all worked up over the rebellious traders of the South. You could tell he was a leader of men and his heart and soul was really into this war. After he was done, my blood was boiling so much I felt like I just needed to hit someone, but I held onto my senses. How was I to know that soon I would be honoring this Major with my services while under his command for the next three years.

Next up was a speaker that everyone in Cattaraugus County respected: Colonel Parker. He was a man who had the confidence as a leader in the community. He was a small man who looked more like a politician than a soldier, but he was smartly dressed in his uniform and spoke with a more deliberate and precise tone than his predecessor. He spoke of our commitment to hold the country together as one nation, and he reminded us that our Constitution was for all the states not just a selected few, who want to pull out if they don't like the laws the majority makes or the way elections are won. He also spoke of what happened to our boys at Bull Run and our need to put an end to this rebellion. He said that without our help, it was possible that the New South could invade us someday and make our lives part of their world if we didn't stop them now. It didn't take me long to decide; I signed up and headed back home before his speech was done.

I made my mind up to just go in and tell Ma flat out what I was doing. It was for our country and our way of life. I didn't want her to know it was also a way for me to see what's out beyond these Allegany Hills and fresh water streams. However, when I arrived home, I went straight to the stable to let Pa know first. He was mucking out the stalls when I entered the barn. After I told him what I had done, he looked concerned, but knew what was burning inside my gut, as he had come to this land from Vermont some 30 years before with the same itch that I had. So he shook his head, as if to understand better and said, "Better go tell your Momma."

I walked up to the house and entered into the kitchen, Ma had just finished clearing the table from the afternoon meal. She was a short woman, not more than four feet ten inches tall and her hair was now more than half grey and braided around the back of her head. Her skin was calloused way beyond her 53 years from the toil of hard labor living on a farm and raising so many offspring. After I finished my words and explained what had transpired, she looked up from the broom she was leaning on. Her eyes were as sad a looking pair as any I have ever seen on a person. For the longest time she didn't say anything and just stared into my eyes. My stomach was churning so much in anticipation of her reaction that I felt as though I would get sick.

Finally, she said calmly, "You're a man now, James, so you've made your decision as a man. I can't hold you here any longer; you just make sure you write and let us know where you are and your condition."

I jumped up from the chair and said, "I will write as often as I possibly can," then kissed her on the forehead and headed back out to the barn to help Pa and make plans to visit Emma Sholtz after supper. Emma is a young lady with whom I have had a good many conversations and who I hold in the highest of regard. She lives a far piece on the same road from our farm towards Conewango, but holding her good looks in my mind makes the long ride worth while. She stands about five feet tall and has the prettiest blond hair I think I have ever seen. Her frame is small, but she holds herself upright very well. We have grown to know each other quite well over the last few years and we have spoken often about our inner most desires.

I waited until after supper and then rode ol' Rumsey over to the farm where Emma lived. As I arrived, she was sitting on a rocking chair on the front porch in a plain blue dress, knitting some kind of a new fancy item for display in the house. She immediately smiled as I dismounted from Rumsey's back

"Well, it's about time you came around for a visit," she said. "I was beginning to wonder if the summer smell from the pig pens was keeping you away."

"Not a chance! Your pigs and ours seem to carry the same perfume this time of the year," I responded, smiling.

She dropped her knitting onto her lap and looked up at me.

"I've missed seeing your face and hearing of your visions, James. You must be very busy over at your place."

"Well Emma," I dropped my head and looked at the floor boards of the porch, "the truth is, I enlisted today and I'll be leaving in a few weeks to go to training camp in Elmira."

She looked into my eyes and said, "So now I guess you'll be beginning this big adventure you've been dreaming about."

It was apparent she was not so happy with me right now, but I was still so excited about venturing outside these mountains, I could not hold it in me any longer. I began to explain to her the need to do one's duty for one's country and to stop the rebellion that is taking place, but somehow, the more I spoke the more she just sat there staring at me and not saying a word.

Finally, I said, "Emma, will you wait for my return?"

She stood up and walked over to me, looked up into my eyes.

"James, you are the only person I think I could tolerate in my life as no other has presented himself with having any brains around here, so I guess I don't have much choice except to wait."

With that, we both laughed and spent the next few hours talking about the new adventure I was about to take.

It took about three weeks to make the arrangements to travel to Elmira with the rest of the boys who signed up at Randolph. There were 43 of us from either the village, town, or from farms surrounding the area that left for Elmira by train that day in early September. It seemed the whole County was there to see us off. They had a small band playing some patriotic music; all the children from the common schools and Randolph Academy were given the day off. Crowley's Store provided refreshments for the event to help with the celebration as their son, Marvel Crowley, was going with us. All the mercantile stores closed their doors this day—even Eddy's Carriage House closed up. The town supervisor gave a speech to everyone and a good time was had by all.

For me, the best part of the whole affair was when Emma arrived with her family. She looked so lovely; her cream-colored face with the little rose cheeks seemed to give me a sense of the pureness she must possess and her smile was such that anyone who accompanied her to a social event would be the envy of the affair. We were able to speak for a while and exchanged our good byes.

"Don't worry," I told her, "I won't be away long— just long enough to see a little of the outside world and put the rebellion to rest."

She nodded in a tender, yet forceful way with her face full of courage. "I will give of myself to the service and happiness of others while you are away, James."

She always carried with her a strong inclination to help others provide a good living on this earth. How little I knew what turmoil and distress this adventure would bring to me and my new friends in the future.

When the 43 of us boarded that train on that warm September day, we left behind a life that would forever be lost to us. For those of us who would return, we would never be the same person we were before we left. As we began to leave the Randolph station, I looked around me at the men who sat within our cabin. There was a mixture of age from the very young, such as myself, to men who were at least in their mid-thirties. I knew about half the men on the train; many were farmers and others were tradesmen from in the village or surrounding areas. I sat next to Frank Jones; he and I were the same age and having met the day we signed up, the journey provided an opportunity to continue with our conversation. He told me he worked at Camp and Adams General Store and that his father was a deacon in his church and he had four brothers and two sisters. For his age, Frank seemed more mature than some of the other boys on the train. He was a plain-looking man who seemed to be actuated by honorable motives. His character lent him to always go about his business in a very deliberate mode. However, he was always in good spirits and spoke with everyone who entered the cabin. He was about six feet tall, with a clear face, dark brown hair and small eyes. He was sort of a lanky individual whose walk reminded me of a long legged stork's strut. He was a very religious type of fellow, but he did not force his beliefs on to anyone and found enjoyment in socializing with the men.

"You know, I signed up to put an end to one man having the right to own another," Frank said. "Father has always said that if God had wanted men to own other men, he would have said so in the Bible."

Personally, I didn't believe this war was about slavery, but more about the greed of the southern people to secede from the very country that fought to free them; but to Frank it was about slavery and only slavery.

We spoke quite a bit about our families and loved ones during the trip to Elmira. I could tell that Frank felt a special passion about this war that I didn't have. He was of a faith that proclaimed slavery to be a sin and it was his goal to free all men from its bondage, even though neither he nor I had never seen a colored man in our lives. It was difficult for me to understand why we should sacrifice our souls to free some other species of mankind to whom I have never laid eyes on.

Sitting directly in front of me, next to the window was Albert Marsh. He was a big man, well over six feet tall with deep eyes that seemed to be constantly staring directly into your mind as if he was determining what type of character you were. His hair was thick and white, and his face clean shaven. He certainly looked much older than his 31 years, but he proclaimed himself to be an old looking young man. During the trip, he told me he worked on a farm his whole life and when his father could no longer farm, the family moved to Randolph, even though he would continue to work as a laborer on the farms surrounding the village. He wasn't married and continued to live with his mother and sister in Randolph. He seemed to be carrying the virtue of making sure he took care of people. He would often turn his head around to face Frank as he spoke in agreement with his convictions to free the slaves.

Sitting next to Albert was Frank Shannon, while Frank was not as outspoken on his convictions about this war, he was a very patriotic individual. His family left Ireland during the great potato famine and understood what it meant to lose one's home country. While he wasn't big on the slavery issue, he was certainly dedicated to the patriotic call to duty to defend the unity of one's country. As he said to us during our ride, "Lads, I've lost one home and have seen a great many of my people die from starvation because of the greed of our Mother Country. I will not again sit back and watch a few destroy the lives of so many without a fight." After he said those words to us, I thought about his sincerity and I knew he was ready for the fight that we sought.

Sitting across from the isle from Frank was Henry Morgan. He was around my age and a person who was full of energy. He was of a smaller stature than most of the farm boys, but it didn't seem to bother him too much. He was not from the Randolph area; instead he originally came from Philadelphia and was staying with his aunt and uncle while attending Randolph Academy when the call went out for more troops. I could tell he was an educated fellow as his words were chosen carefully and his knowledge of the world was greater than the rest of us. He didn't seem to have a conviction one way or the other about the slavery issue; he was joining because he didn't want to be left behind.

However, he did say, "I have seem many a Black man in Philadelphia and can say without reservation that they do not possess the wherewithal to make anything of themselves except as common laborers. But the separation of the country—now that is another matter entirely. We cannot allow ourselves to be bullied by rich plantation owners who want to have all the say in what our country does and that is why we need to stop their rebellion."

Thanks to Henry, the trip was never without talk and I think we were all glad when the train pulled into the Elmira station. As we prepared to disembark from the train, I noticed how large the station was. All around us were masses of people, both military and civilian. It was as if we were in Randolph multiplied 100 times. An officer dressed in uniform came towards us and announced that all men arriving for military service were to line up in twos behind him. As we made our way to position ourselves accordingly, I noticed a young man who seemed to be somewhat confused and bewildered as to where to go, so I went over and offered to line up with him. His name was David Cooper and he told me he was 22 years old and lived on a farm west of Randolph, along the Jamestown Road. He was a scrawny, tall fellow, barely 130 pounds and spoke with a stutter. Just as we were beginning to have a conversation, the officer yelled out for us to follow him and start walking towards the camp. Along the way, David told me he had to leave home as things were bad for his family. His father was not much of a farmer, having immigrated to Randolph from Ireland via the docks of New York. The farm on which they lived did not produce enough food to sustain their large family, so he decided to join up and go where he would be fed and clothed, and relieve his family of that burden. He too, often remembered the hard times of a poor growing season and through his broken speech would speak of some incidents that had occurred. I felt as if he was lacking some confidence and seemed somewhat timid in his advance to meet new people, for he knew no one else on the train. I decided to keep an eye on him until he settled in.

Once we arrived at Camp Elmira, we were taken aback by the size and number of men who had arrived from our county. We were given quarters within barracks number three. The buildings were made of rough lumber and only had a few windows where light could find its way in. The beds were made of hard boards with feedbags filled with pine needles and straw as a softener. There were eight men to a room in the barracks, it was decided the five of us on the train, along with my recently acquired new friend, David Cooper, would room together. There would be two others to join us to whom I had seen in the village previously, but did not know them very well.

We slept that night and early next morning we found ourselves being formed into a regiment consisting of all members from Cattaraugus County. The 43 of us who traveled by train together would be part of Company B of the 64th New York Regiment. The two other boys in our room were Lemuel Owen, about 30 years old who sported a mustache. He had what seemed to me to be reddish colored hair, which he combed over his head in long lengths from a low parting. He was a likable guy, full of good natured energy; was built in a solid frame for his average height and he was absolutely the most caring of his personal belongings as anyone I have ever seen. He said he was from Conewango and married, with a very young daughter named Ina. He was a surveyor by trade and a farmer by necessity when there was no work to be had. Then there was Franklin Higbe; he was around my age, a little less than six feet tall with a very stocky frame. He also was very likable and came with a personality of concern for the wellbeing of the rest of us. He told me his family moved to Samples Hill outside the village of Randolph from Albion, New York. He had nine brothers and sisters and loved to cook for them all. Franklin worked in the tannery at the Village and was of a likable disposition. For the next week, we would all begin learning a soldier's life, take our oath of allegiance to the Army, and with the exception of being somewhat bored every once in a while, we were not too badly off.

The eight of us began to meld together more at each passing day. We would eat our meals together, marching to the eating houses two abreast. The food served was passed around a large wooden table made of rough sawed pine. Dishpans were used to pass the potatoes while pie tins were used for the beef and pork. Bread was in a large basket and already buttered. There were times in the early days when the food didn't seem to be fit for consumption, but the Colonel told us to be patient as the cooks were not cooks before joining up and they were still learning their jobs.

As each week progressed, our boys from Randolph became closer to one another and especially the eight of us sharing the same barracks. We were given our blue uniforms, which excited everyone—especially those whose own threads were thin and ready to fall off. We drilled and marched everyday to the instructions of the Drill Masters who were veterans of the Mexican War. No one considered himself a soldier until he learned to march and use his weapons. After a few weeks of training, it was time for the boys in our company (numbering 82) to choose our leaders. This process would take about a week after those who wanted to be leaders announced their intentions. As in all elections, those who were running for leadership positions were elected by popularity and not by how they were as a leader.

During the next four months, we would march, fire our weapons, cook, perform guard duty, and wash our uniforms. We received the issuance of equipment and it was one of the utmost significant events of our stay. Then we had to carry this equipment on our bodies as we marched: a gun, waist belt for bayonet, cap box, cartage box and belt across the left shoulder, knapsacks, and haversacks for provisions, canteens holding three pints of water, plate, cup, knife, and fork. Our days would be filled with rigorous exercises, sometimes to the extreme detriment of why we signed up according to our way of thinking.

We had to learn the meaning of the distinctive calls sounded by the buglers or tapped out by the drummer boys equaling about a dozen. It would start at around 6:00 in the morning with a call to Reveille. This was our signal to roll out, dress and muster for morning roll call. While our barracks seemed to be always dressed and on time, there were others who found it hard to rise and fell into their places with only one shoe on or stood shivering in their linens. We stood ludicrously in rank, and a succession of short, dry coughs always ran up and down the line. After the sergeant of each company called the roll, we would be allowed to return briefly to our quarters to complete our dressing.

About 30 minutes later came the breakfast call known as "Peas on a Trencher." No one was late here. Franklin Higbe was one who knew his food and was always the first in line from our barracks and he would test each item as he went through the line giving us an up or down vote with his thumb indicating how we will feel from our consumption this day. Thirty more minutes, then sick call was sounded for the ailing and fatigued. They were lined up and marched to the surgeon for examination. If bedridden, the surgeon would visit them at their quarters. Fatigue duty meant policing the grounds, digging drainage ditches or cutting wood—but no marching.

At about 8 o'clock, guard-mounting call rang out, at which time the first sergeant of each company turned out his detail for the next 24 hours of guard duty. The next call was for drill, which commonly lasted until the dinner or when the "Roast Beef" call was rendered. Then came some free time until the latter part of the afternoon when we had additional drilling, followed by a dress parade of the entire company. This usually led to retreat call, followed by supper call, followed not long after by tattoo call, where another roll call was taken. When the final call of the day was sounded, it signaled "lights out, noises cease and all men to their quarters."

We had many visitors to the camp, both relatives and girlfriends. Emma could not make the trip, but during our four months in Elmira I was able to obtain a furlough for a few days and went home to visit everyone. But, as each week passed by, our non-movement to join the rest of the Army began to give way to discontent amongst the men and it was starting to show in the shortness of tempers towards our leaders. One night, the eight of us, thoroughly bored with just sitting around, decided to make a dash past the guards and head for town. We were able to have one of our fellow company members draw the attention of the gate guards as we quickly dashed through the line and to the road to town. We had just received our first pay draw as soldiers and we were anxious to enjoy some of the fruits of the city of Elmira before our departure.

Before we left camp, there was an issue that needed to be resolved. A thief had been infecting our company and the men were fed up with him, so a trap was set by Franklin Higbe. When the trap was sprung and the culprit caught, we took it upon ourselves to deal with his deceit. J.P. Willis was his name and he was from New York City. We shaved his head, poured tar over him, wrote thief on his back and paraded him off to the regimental headquarters. We made it known to all: no toleration of thievery would be accepted within our company.

Now, we could go to town with satisfaction. It was during this first trip to town that energies of confinement were released and the personalities gave way to the temptations of one's soul. David Cooper was the first to find the sign for the "Old Spring Tavern," located just inside the city limits. As we walked in we were surprised to see many of our fellow soldiers from the 64th on furlough or on the same sneak march as us and enjoying the liquids of desire. The owner of the Tavern, a Mr. Joshua Rich was a friendly sort and welcomed all soldiers to his establishment, offering not only his locally brewed drink, but games of chance and visits to his private rooms with one of his employed fair maidens if you were willing to forego two dollars of your pay. There were also musicians performing patriotic songs and many a soldier sang himself sober. A few of us began to partake in the many games of Bluff or Chuck-a-Luck being played. Frank Shannon, who acknowledged to me some time ago of his long desire to experience the feeling of enjoyment in the arms of a fair maiden, selected one of the awaiting maidens and made off to a room. It was the first time I had seem him so determined to achieve a goal since we arrived here.

While we waited for his report, David Cooper and Henry Morgan were thoroughly enjoying the tavern's drink. Their speech was of a constant nature and so loud they seemed to be yelling at each other. Frank Jones did not drink, but he did sit and enjoy the rest of us making fools of ourselves. Albert Marsh was one who drank a bit, but was always looking over his shoulder for a danger sign as if he were acting as a Mother Goose over the rest of us. Lemuel Owen, Franklin Higbe and I sat, drank, and enjoyed having many conversations about our home, families, and our desire to get to the war as soon as possible. The one thing we all did well was enjoy the company of Mr. Rich and large quantities of his beer.

Finally, it was past the time to head back to camp, Frank Shannon seemed to be fully blushed as he exited the room of delight. He'd only been in there for just over a ten-minute stay, but the smile on his face indicated his venture was satisfactory to him. He then proceeded to down many pints of cheer and inform us of his first affair and details of the ritual. David Cooper was in a sad drunken shape also, and in need of a leaning post to get him moving in the right direction. As we approached the guards surrounding our camp, we ducked into the woods to our left. Albert Marsh motioned for us to keep our voices quiet, but that was quite impossible for David Marsh and Henry Morgan. Both these individuals had great difficulty holding their speech when they were sober let alone in their current condition. We sat there for about ten minutes, but it seemed like an hour waiting for the guards to be distracted. Finally they moved to go for a walk to their right, which was good for us. We dashed as best we could across the open lanes and back to our quarters and slept like logs until the next morning.

CHAPTER 2
Camp Fenton

The concerns of the men must have had an impact on our leaders, as we learned that our regiment would be finally moving out on December 10 to Washington D.C. We drew three days rations for our dispatch to the nation's capitol; they consisted of two loaves of bread and a pound and a half of beef or mutton. We boarded the train around 5:00 in the evening; the sun would be setting and thus by the time the Northern Central Railroad cars started rolling toward the Susquehanna River Valley and their rendezvous with history, the regiment would not have noticed any of the landmarks along their way that would influence their lives during the impending struggle. As our train passed through Harrisburg en-route to Baltimore delivering my now eager civilian friends-turned-fighters, I wondered how this rail would serve otherwise as a principal conduit of supplies.

As we wound around the Susquehanna Valley, it crossed bridges in the city of Harrisburg and the little towns of Columbia and Wrightsville. I wasn't sure if I was daydreaming or dreaming during my winks of sleep I was able to catch, but thoughts were going through my mind as to how many men this Iron Horse with its blue-clad human cargo, crossed over these critical links between the north and south in the recent past.

We arrived in Baltimore on December 11th and disembarked with loaded weapons as we marched through the streets. We were warned of "plug-uglies" possibly being there lying in wait to attack us. However, these southern sympathizers were nowhere to be found. Instead, our reception was welcoming as we were intercepted at the depot by generous-hearted women with sandwiches and hot coffee. The short trip from Baltimore to Washington was delayed until the wee hours of the morning, thus providing the first glimpse of our nation's capitol at daybreak on the 12th. I remember we could see the grand outlines of the capitol building and as we approached, its grandeur and beauty grew upon us. Perhaps it seemed more grand and beautiful to us because its possession was at that time seriously threatened. As we disembarked just outside the capitol, we could see in the distance a rebel flag plainly flying from their outpost at Arlington, Virginia, from its unfinished dome. The Capitol was protected by perhaps 50 to 60 camps surrounding the entire city; our camp was to be located near the Virginia line across from Arlington.

We marched into an area where it was designated we would set up our camp, which we would call Camp Fenton, named after R.E. Fenton, our Congressman representing Cattaraugus County. While we stayed there, he would visit us from time to time giving us a taste of his views in a speech. He was a soldier's advocate, constantly supporting bills to expedite or increase military benefits. He would go on to be elected Governor of New York in 1864 with the help from many absentee soldiers' ballot.

Our camp ground was relatively flat so our wedge tent ends could fit evenly with the ground to help hold water from draining in when it rained. There would be four men to a tent, so we divided ourselves up and placed the two tents side be side. Lemuel Owen, Frank Shannon, and Henry Morgan were in my tent, leaving the other four friends beside us. These were only temporary housing for us, as our first duty was to build a log hut for all eight of us using both logs as a base and our tents as a roof, filling in the holes with mud. Our fireplace was built from wood and mud combined, requiring constant attention when lit. I wrote home a lot during this time. I would often think of Emma and become homesick to see her. Her letters would always lift me up out of any slump I might be in. She always presented herself as the "Lady in Waiting" and I always presented myself as her "Soldier of Fortune."

Lemuel Owen and I became very close during this time. A very neat and meticulous person, he would talk to me of his wife and one-year-old daughter back home. He would sit for hours reading over and over her letters as if he were thinking of what to say in response. Then, after a few hours, he would pick up pen and paper and begin to write down his response. While his letters seemed to be few and far between, he cherished each one separately and stored them as carefully as he did his personal belongings.

Once we were set up in our camp, the daily routines started again, the only exception was our picket duty was for real as we were placed on Virginia soil just south of the Capitol. A few times we were sent on reconnaissance to gather information on enemy positions. There were always shady characters among the soldiers of all camps and we were camping amongst a group of them. Peddlers, wives, girlfriends, and relatives were a constant addition to our camp life. The peddlers were the worst—they would buy cheap or steal their wares and then sell them at exorbitant prices to the new green soldiers.

One night, I thought I heard faint sounds from far away and tried to wake my sleepy eyes to investigate, but they were difficult to open as we had drilled hard that day. Finally, I opened my eyes after Franklin Higbe emitted one of his characteristic snores, a malignant mix of whistles and buzzing. Frank Shannon was sleeping on his right side; his linen underdrawers were soaked with sweat. I was thinking about reaching over to poke Franklin and silence him when the sound separated into recognizable elements, night insects and something else. I held my breath and didn't move. Even with my cheek pressed against the camp bed, I could see the tent entrance open. A silhouette momentarily blocked the glow of the guardpost lantern. I heard the intruder breathing; he was inside and looking for something. He was going through Franklin's trousers looking for his money as we had just been paid that day. I was in a hard position from which to rise suddenly, but I did it anyway, bolting up from the waist, I let out a growl I hoped would confuse and frighten the thief. Instead it woke Franklin and he immediately took a lunge at the shadowy man who had grabbed his money from his pocket.

"Hey, give me that," yelled Franklin. The thief then drove an elbow into Franklin's face and blood spurted from his left nostril. Franklin staggered and the thief dived into the street of neatly spaced tents and raced left, away from the picket post where the lanterns shone. Bleeding and swearing, Franklin and the others in our tent went after him. We could pick out a few details of the thief's appearance. He was heavy and wore white gaiters, the same worn by the peddlers throughout the camp.

The thief's arms and legs pumped quickly as we and Franklin ran in pursuit while blood trickled down his upper lip, but he just spat the blood away. Stones and burrs were hurting our bare feet as we pursued, but we were gaining. The thief looked back, his face a round red, then I heard Franklin holler just as he hurled himself forward, his feet leaving the ground a second before his hands caught the waist of the thief's bloomers. The man screamed an obscenity; both men fell with Franklin landing on the back of the man's legs, badly jarred. The thief dropped the money and struggled to turn beneath Franklin and get free, kicking all the while. A gaitered boot knocked Franklin's head back and the thief began to jump up. Dazed, Franklin grabbed the man's left leg and pulled him down to the ground again, the thief then pulled out a huge bowie knife from his belt sheath. Franklin turned his head to avoid a cut that would have sliced his face. We were now approaching and yelling "Corporal of the Guard, Corporal of the Guard," and with us coming closer and causing more attention, the thief tried to jump up to run when Franklin punched him in his privates. The thief buckled, his arms dropped to the ground and so did his knife; Franklin picked it up and drove the blade straight into his right thigh. We all then pounced on him and held him down until the guards arrived. An officer finally arrived and questioned us as to what happened and then had the peddler hauled off to the surgeon first and then to a session with leg irons and chains.

In our camp there were plenty of scallywags, trying to get at our boys' money as easily as possible. Finally, we thought we had rid the camp of one of the worst of the bunch, until we found another. One night Franklin Higbe and I went to a artillery camp nearby and borrowed a long rope. Upon reaching the targeted peddler's tent and making sure he was sound asleep, we circled his tent with the rope like an Ox bow. On the count of three, we both pulled the rope and the tent and all its hanging wares came to the ground and it was a mess with wares scattered everywhere. The peddler left camp the next morning, knowing full well we were tired of his misusing the "green" boys in blue. It sent a message to future peddlers wanting to set up their tents to watch the 64th; be fair or suffer the consequences.

The winter passed slowly and during the next few months we visited all the places in our nation's Capital. Furloughs were few and far between as we were considered "green" soldiers with mostly all the furloughs going to the veterans. Frank Shannon was having the time of his life every chance he could. One night I think he visited three brothels before we returned to our camp. I was starting to become a little concerned about the health of a few of our boys around the middle of March in 1862. David Cooper was drinking pretty heavily, most every day, from the poorly made whiskey he was buying from the peddlers. At one point, he was caught drunk while on duty by the Captain. He was made to walk around for three days inside an empty beer barrel. From that time on, he was more careful when and where he drank, but he still consumed a fair amount.

Frank Shannon seemed to be wearing out after a few drill sessions, his face looked drawn and withered. I thought he had contracted the measles as it was going through our camp like a wild fire; many of us had at least a mild case of it. But he didn't have any spots on him and he wouldn't go to the surgeon.

He came to me one day and said "James, I don't rightly know what ails me, but my inners is like a boiling pot today and I need you to cover for me at muster."

"Frank, why don't you go on sick call, you may have seen too many brothels and have caught yourself a bad dose of indignation," I replied.

"I can't," he said as he prepared to return to his blanket on the floor, "I don't want to be separated from our group, and I don't feel comfortable with anyone else."

So when Franks name was called, I replied "Here" while he slept and his illness worsened. I thought maybe he had gotten some bad food, but that would have only lasted a few days until you expelled the evil, but Frank has been sick for over three weeks now and I am quite concerned. Our food was adequate, but many times we had to cook our own meals, using our tin cups to boil the raw pork we were given with our biscuits. Finally, towards the end of March, we received orders that we were going to move south. Excitement filtered throughout the camp; what we have been waiting some six months for was about to begin.

During the winter I kept track of the 43 men who boarded the train with us in Randolph the previous September. Three of our fellows were discharged from Washington in January and one in March; they all had bad cases of the measles, which found its way into their lungs. They were in poor condition and could not go on. So when we left Camp Fenton, we had 39 of the 43 men marching to our destiny. Our Regiment was at full force when we left to start our long trip to old Virginia on April 5, 1862. The 64th Regiment was assigned to General Howard's 1st Brigade, Richardson's 1st Division, II Corp. under General Sumner. As we began to travel on the Steamer, Frank Shannon was starting to feel real bad; he had the shakes and was sweating all the time. When we landed at the first land stations on Virginia soil at the village of Hampton, he could no longer avoid the separation from us; the surgeons ordered him off to the hospital tents.

CHAPTER 3
Battle of Fair Oaks

Hampton Virginia would be called Ft. Monroe and it was located where the James River meets the Chesapeake. We would camp here for a few weeks as most of the Army was in advance of us and their movement up the Peninsula was in a slow prodding way, always with advanced cavalry looking for the enemy along the way. Every day while we were camped here, one of us would go up to the hospital tents to see Frank Shannon. David Cooper came back one time and said he was looking better, while Frank Jones and Albert Marsh both said he was looking worse. The last day I saw him was on April 16th. The hospital tent was full of men who looked to be in bad shape from the same infection that was griping Frank. He was very weak and thinning, his mouth seemed to be parched, but the doctor told us it was his body withdrawing from the disease. The doctor had told me he had a combination of illnesses; he must have eaten some bad meat along the way giving him consumption and he had a venereal disease—both were attacking his organs. I stood next to him along with

Lemuel Higbe and Henry Morgan. We tried to our best to raise his spirits, but staring death in the face is a difficult task for anyone. We stayed for a few hours more.

He looked at us and said, "Boys, I have a feeling my number may be up on this world and I want you to know I never met any finer group of men than you, boys. When you get back to Randolph, will you look up my family and let them know I was a good soldier?"

"Of course," we all answered him. When we left, little was said amongst the three of us as we made our way to our own tents. I spoke with the other boys and made them aware of Frank's condition. That night, by the campfire, there was little conversation as each of us went about the business of making preparations for the fight ahead; we had not yet fought one battle, but we already have felt the pain of war inside our hearts. Everyone was holding their heads down.

The next morning, we got word that Frank had died during the night and his body probably would be claimed by his family in Randolph. It was also the day we received orders to prepare to move out as the Army had established an even flow now on the roads heading toward Richmond and the future fight that could end this war and allow me to go home to Emma. As we left, I took a quick count of the original 43 men and I noted we were now down to 38. We had already suffered a 10 percent loss without an angry shot being fired.

Over the next few weeks, we would march 10–15 miles, camp, set up our pickets, and continue to move deeper into the mouth of the serpent called "Virginia." We all noticed the people of this region were a lot different than where we came from; they seemed to be a lot more ignorant. At camp one night, Franklin Higbe was telling us he had asked a farm woman who was standing along the road, "How far is Richmond?"

She replied through her black teeth as she spit out her chew, "Well right smart distance I reckon."

He further asked of her, "Is it a lot of miles?"

To which she replied, "What's a mile?"

He told us he just moved on, thinking how stupid the people were here.

"What did this fair maiden look like?"

"She was sharp-nosed, tobacco chewing, snuff-rubbing, flax-headed, hatchet-faced, yellow-eyed, sallow-skinned, cotton-dressed, flat-breasted, bare-headed, long-wasted, hump-shouldered, stoop-necked, big-footed, straddle-toed, sharp-shinned, thin-lipped, pale-faced, lantern-jawed, sill-looking damsel!"

We all laughed aloud at his description of this poor woman.

Word had spread that we were approaching Richmond and it would not be long before our long awaited fight would begin. On May 30th, our II Corp. under General Sumner had reached the northern banks of the Chickahominy River and was waiting for the order for us to come across the grapevine bridge that we had helped to build. The IV Corp had arrived at Seven Pines, about three miles east of Richmond.

The IV Corp stretched their lines from the left of the Williamsburg road across and to the right side as far as possible with Fair Oaks being in the center. They were fortifying their position there with a strong line of rifle pits. The III Corp. was ordered to take position at White Oak swamp south and east of Seven Pines to guard the left side and rear of the rest of the Army. On the same morning as these positions were being established, rebel reconnaissance discovered the rifle pits and reported to their General Johnston by noon that a strong force of Federals were approaching from the south side of the Chickahominy.

General Johnston had charge of the protection of the city of Richmond; he had already heard that General McDowell's Corp. of 40,000 men were marching southeast from the Virginia Valley to hook up with McClelland's Army of the Potomac. This amount of force would surely defeat his small Army; therefore, he needed to delay McClelland and McDowell from hooking up until he was reinforced by Generals Jackson and Beauregard. He was determined to strike at McClelland early and cause him to stop. On the night of the 30th of May, the IV Corp. captured an aide to Johnston and heard the movement of trains with many cars during the night giving more suspicion to the movement of enemy troops to a position directly in front of them.

While the Federals were aware of these troop movements, we were not in the ready position to defend a large scale attack as yet. Luckily, owing to a severe storm on the night of the 30th there was confusion in the Confederate ranks in moving their troops to their positions and they did not begin their attack until around 1 o'clock on the 31st. At about noon a scout rode back to our General Casey's headquarters with word that the enemy was approaching in force on the Williamsburg road. As the III and IV Corp. began to bring their men into position to do battle, word was relayed back throughout the rest of the Army of the oncoming battle.

Our company was placed in the ready to move our position early in the morning. When General Sumner received the order at 2:30 in the afternoon to move his two divisions across the river to support the III and IV Corp. we were already in marching order. As we were going along in double step, I couldn't help but feel the adrenaline flowing through my veins like the rapids of a river. My thoughts were all over the place with the excitement. This is what I have been waiting for. Will I be brave enough? Can I really kill a man? Will I be killed? What about Emma? I have to make Ma proud of me. Fortunately, today our division arrived at the battlefield at 4 o'clock in the afternoon just as the enemy was retiring; too late to take part in today's engagement; too late to taste the sweetness of the fight upon my lips.

We made camp on the very spot at which we arrived at the field of battle. The enemy had retreated through the woods from which they came and were about a mile away according to our scouts. Pickets were established and fires were built. We were given three days rations with instructions to cook the meat immediately and thoroughly to conserve the nourishment. We were each given 60 rounds of ammunition; only 40 rounds could be carried in the leather cartridge boxes on our belt, the others would have to be carried in our pockets. We were also given the same amount of percussion caps; we then cleaned our muskets of all debris and moisture. We were told to make sure our canteens were full, as water would be scarce tomorrow.

Even though we secured our tents, no one slept much this night. Henry Morgan's voice was in constant motion and as he filled the air with words of battle anticipation for us all, it was easy to realize that all our nerves were frazzled. Albert Marsh and Frank Jones went about the business of finding from others in the regiment what our position might be in the morning. At 2:00 am, a General's War Conference was held at Sumner's camp and the strategies for the next day were laid out.

About 4:00 am, the first sergeant came by shouting, "Up boys, the enemy will soon be here. I can see their bayonets glittering on the hills and smell their unclean bodies coming every so closer."

We sprang to our feet in unison; coffee and food were served in a hastily manner, then we were ordered to form up in twos and make ready to move to our designated ground. It was a clear night, with the moon at three quarters, stars were easily seen and it reminded me of many a summers night spent back home, which seemed so far away right now. As we marched to our designation position, many thoughts of home and Emma were going through my mind. A day like this day back home, I might be sitting on a good size turkey waiting for him to poke his head high enough for me to take it off. But these thoughts were quickly put away and I tried to replace them with visions of courage I will need very shortly when told to fire upon and kill another human being.

We were placed in a line of twos at the edge of the woods along the Williamsburg road just to the right of the 81st Pennsylvania. Our officers were going up and down the lines with their sabers drawn giving instructions. Our Colonel spoke to us as he walked by.

"Men, the hour for which you have so eagerly awaited has arrived. We are about to engage the enemy. Let every man do his duty, be cool. Keep your ranks. If any of your comrades fall, do not stop to help them; leave them to the care of the men who have been specially detailed for removal of the wounded. The best way to protect the wounded, and yourselves as well, is to press forward and drive the enemy from the field. Hold your fire until the Rebels are in easy range, then aim low, fire deliberately. Close steadily on the enemy, and when you get within charging distance, rush on him with the bayonet. If you do this, you are sure to win."

After his speech, I felt as if I needed to unload my stomach in front of everyone. I had never before felt such a sickness as this. Sweat was protruding from my entire body and I wiped my brow many times with my coat sleeve. I then looked over at Lemuel Owen to my left and David Cooper to my right and both of them were sweating also, their mouths were wide and their breathing was quick. Franklin Higbe's hands were shaking so much, he had to grab tight to his musket to stop the sight of the trembling. Albert Marsh stared ahead as if he was trying to see any images through the breaking of darkness of the early morning.

My throat and lips seemed to be parched and my chest felt as if a 50 pound stone was resting on it. I noticed my breathing was heavy and I felt as if my eyeballs were about to explode from my face. I looked over to Frank Jones and saw him on one knee giving a prayer to the almighty. I hoped he was praying for all of us, for we are about to enter an unknown arena filled with uncertainty and danger. I thought about the test awaiting us, I was not so much afraid of death or injury as I was of perhaps my inability to stand up under the awful and unknown test of inner strength that lay ahead. Better a thousand times to fall facing the enemy, than to play the coward and bring humiliation or shame to our company and folks back home.

The time was now 5:00 am and we could see the silhouette of Cavalry men on the horizon; this was followed by a small body of skirmishers sent out to test the location of our lines. A few shots of artillery sent them back out of sight. The sound grew quiet once more and I knew we were within minutes of opening the dance. My thoughts were drawn to Emma and how much I wished I could be with her just one more time. I wished I had written to her last night; now she may never know of my thoughts of her before this battle.

In what seemed like an eternity, but was actually only a few minutes, a massive force of Confederates emerged from the woods and immediately opened fire with heavy musketry. We were given the command to "Forward, march!" As we moved, I could feel my legs falter as if they were reluctant to hold me up, but somehow I managed to keep them going. Officers kept shouting the words "Center, dress!" "Close up the ranks!" Bullets were now flying over our heads and buzzing past our ears. We still had not reached our position of battle of about 20 yards to the edge of the woods. Right in front of us men from the Pa regiment were falling to the ground in bundles. One man grunted as if he's been punched in the stomach. He just sat down and gazed ruefully ahead, his eyes had an indefinite reproach and a surprised look; another man who was shot in the knee dropped his rifle and clung to a tree with both arms, desperately crying for help. God knows how I managed to ignore these cries of my fellow comrades and continue forward. I concentrated on watching for movement in the fog of smoke just ahead—all the while stepping over the dead and around the wounded whose screams became an echo in the arena as the cannons and musketry noise continuously filled the air.

We finally reached our position and the restraint from not being able to fire our guns in retaliation was almost too much to bear. When we were finally given the command to fire, it would come as a tremendous relief of carrying such a heavy burden. Now, the fear seems to have left, I fell to the ground, rolled over and began to reload, tearing open the black powder cartridges with my teeth as quickly as possible. Once the ram was in, I stood up, fired again in the direction of the enemy and immediately fell back down to reload once more, rising to advance a small portion and firing once more.

After about half an hour we were successful in stopping the enemies advance upon us. Then there was a lull in the firing as the Rebel forces fell back to reform. Some of the men in our regiment began to cheer frenziedly while many others just fell silent, trying to gather themselves together. It was at this time I looked around at some of the comrades I could recognize and noticed their faces looked as though they had been changed to the worst image of the Devil as I had ever seen. Each one had black powder spewed from the mouths to their eyelids and look as spirits of death when both of their eyes were totally opened. My blood seemed to cool a bit and my spirit began to slip away somewhat; I became aware of the foul smell from the atmosphere in which we had been struggling in and found myself dripping like a laborer in the foundry. I grasped my canteen and took a big swallow as I watched a few of the men unable to steal themselves to a continuance of the ordeal take advantage of the interval and slip away to the rear. Others tried, and officers quickly closed the ranks with file closers. Our entire Brigade was again ordered to move forward, then we heard the order to "fix bayonets" and steel would grate against steel as the sharp instruments were fitted over the ends of the rifle barrels. The order to "forward march" was announced and we started moving towards the rebels, who were still trying to reform their lines, but were in complete disarray. Then it was "Charge!" and we started running towards them yelling as loudly as our lungs could manage. It was enough to force the rebels into total retreat, throwing away their rifles, hats and coats as they ran back towards Richmond through the woods from which they emerged.

We did not pursue their retreat and were ordered to return the point of where we started. The first battle was over and the feeling of exhilaration was flowing quickly through our veins until we came upon the wounded and dead lying in front of us on our return. I recognized Albert and asked if he had been hit, he said not, but then he looked at me.

"David Cooper took a ball early and is no longer with us," he said. I couldn't believe my ears, what was he talking about?, David was on my right when we formed up originally, I may have lost track of him during all the excitement, but I heard no scream, and I saw no bullet take him down. Albert continued, "David was to my left and he fell in front of me as we began our march to the edge of the woods, a bullet hit him in the head just before we were ordered to shoot our first round.

I couldn't believe it, he fell next to me and I didn't even know it. My concentration was totally on myself. O my God, how could this have happened and I not notice? Maybe there was something I could have done for him. On the way back through the woods we found David, he was laying face up with what was left of his head, his eyes were still open. A rebel bullet had found their mark right in his forehead; he was killed instantly. He would no longer enjoy the fruits of his drink; neither will we enjoy his quirky laid-back approach to life itself. He will be missed tremendously for no person can replace his soul within our inner circle of friendship.

Now our original eight is down to six and our regiment suffered heavily as well with 173 men either wounded or killed here. Of the original 43 men from Randolph in Company B, we had two killed and two wounded. Those wounded will now be discharged and sent home. Of the original 43 men of September 7 of the previous year, we now had 34 left. But this fight was not yet over. Our regiment was ordered to move in reserve of the Army. We received orders to move to Gaines Mills, which was about four miles northeast from our location, we assumed it would be to re-form our Army to push forward to capture Richmond and end this war. But as we arrived here, we found the entire Army had been ordered here and we were shaped in a semi circle in front of Gaines Mill stretching in a line from Glendale and Malvern Hill.

From this point we stayed from June 3 until June 25; we set up defenses and established pickets completely around our camps with skirmishers out in front of our lines. Our main force of about 60,000 men was safely behind us—about five miles. Often during a firelight chat, many of us couldn't understand why we pulled back from our position at Fair Oaks when we had the Rebels on the run. Henry Morgan was exceedingly upset, and during these private chats he would claim our General to be weak and afraid to attack. I spent quite a lot of time writing to the folks back home of our experiences thus far; I especially wrote to Emma to let her know I made it through the first test of courage that each man in this regiment must make. After a week at this location, the heat and humidity began to take its toll. Some days it was almost unbearable and I began to wonder how any human being could survive in this climate. Mosquitoes were rampant and sickness was taking many fighting men out of the ranks. It seemed to me we would be taking far less casualties fighting off the Rebels than fighting off the disease.

How little did we know the enemy was being reinforced during this time by Beauregard's Army and Jackson's command from the Shenandoah Valley. During our time of regrouping, the rebels were able to amass an Army the size of ours. They also had a new leader, General Robert E. Lee. He replaced General Joe Johnston who had been wounded at Fair Oaks. Nothing happened for three weeks. We weren't aware that our Commander, General McClelland had written a letter to the President asking for more men to continue his attack; he was up against a more superior force in number and was placing upon the President the responsibility of our loss if he did not conduct the war as the General saw fit.

On June 25th, all the politicking would end as our Army was attacked in a minor clash at Oak Grove while we were attempting to move siege guns closer to drive back the Confederate pickets there. The next day there was a large attack at Mechanicsville by A. P. Hill's forces against McCall's brigade resulting in two hours of heavy fighting. Porter's brigade came up to assist McCall and drove back the Rebels with heavy casualties. McClelland, sensing this was a diversionary attack where he was seriously outnumbered, withdrew his own position to the southeast and safety.

The next day, it was our turn in the box. The "band of six," as we now called ourselves were among the many that were bunkered down behind our breastworks and trenches when the attack came. To our left was a swamp terrain, which protected us from being outflanked by infantrymen. A. P. Hill brought his entire force against our right flank and as we were entrenched on the far left; we could do little to help. However, our boys held off the attackers and they retreated back and all was calm again for awhile. The day was hot, so much so that our canteens were half empty before noon and we hadn't fired a single shot. It was about 3:30 in the afternoon, at the height of the most immense heat of the day that we were hit head on by a strong force from Longstreet's command. Pickett led the attack and our entire line was able to contribute to the response. It was a severe fire with heavy losses on both sides, but Pickett was beaten back. Just following this attack General Slocum's division arrived to help our defense as someone yelled out "Here they come again," but this time the attack was from Jackson's Army. Again, they concentrated on the center of our line and again they were repulsed after about half an hour of fighting.

About 8 o'clock that evening, we were all feeling a little too relaxed, as we thought we would not see another attack until the next day. But they came at us again during the night hours. This time the rebels came again and again and kept hitting the center of our line as hard as they could. Not being fully prepared for such an attack, our line started to collapse from the Texas brigade's constant pounding. They opened a gap in our line and came onto the field; it was Pickett's men for their second go round of the day. This time they broke the middle and we all knew we had to retreat and fast or else many of us would face the risk of capture or being killed. Our group was one of the last to withdraw and we were on a full run in the dark of night. Thank God those who had fled ahead of us had already trampled out a path; following it made our progress a little easier.

I followed the path until I caught up with someone blocking it. It was a tiny soldier lying dead, his hands holding on to the blue painted rim of a drum. I reached over for the narrow shoulders of the drummer boy, caught hold and flung the boy to one side, but not before I saw the glare in the youngster's opened eyes. My panic now grew worse as I plunged through thicker trees and across a creek. I heard shells whining in so close I leaped to a tree and threw my arms around it and was yelling, "O God, no!" as the shell exploded. It must have been a few minutes later when I came to and heard the cries in the dark, the moans and sudden shrieks. I started to grope everywhere on my body, feeling for injuries. Once I realized I was without injury, I dropped to my knees and began to crawl. I bumped my head against tree trunks and crawled through some vicious briars, but finally, the ground sloped downward and I smelled the water ahead. I began to crawl faster, my hands sinking into the mud, but my mouth was totally parched and I had to begin to drink. I scooped the water up with both hands, but it tasted real bad, causing me to throw up. I stood up and began following the stream tripping over bodies and bobbing heads as I go. I now came upon a small creek path and quickly ran along it, snorting and running in my own urine soaked trousers as fast as I could, when I finally found the main road and caught up to one of our units, I realized our pursuers had stopped.

By four in the morning we had withdrawn across the Chickahominy, burning the bridges behind us. When General McClelland, who was establishing a new supply base along the James River, heard of this defeat, he ordered the entire Army to move to Harrison's landing. He decided to abandon his advance on Richmond and begin the retreat. His arrogance stood out as he wrote to the Secretary of War, "If I save this Army now I tell you plainly that I owe no thanks to you or any other persons in Washington—you have done your best to sacrifice the Army." He left for Harrison's landing, leaving no instructions or a second in Command for the next three battles, while our Army retreated. For the remainder of the retreat to Harrison's landing he had no further communications with the Army fronts.

CHAPTER 4
Harrison's Landing

As our company made its way to Harrison's Landing, we all felt demoralized. How could we do so well in our first battle and be in the condition we are now. Our march was exceedingly gruesome; some of us could hardly continue on as we had been awake now for at least two days. However, we couldn't stop, for stopping meant the possibility of capture and to think about giving up our freedom gave us the motivation to keep going. We had to march about 20 miles to the southeast and many of the men carried wounds with them as they departed. The more severely wounded were left at the mercy of the enemy and hopefully, they would be treated humanely. I found myself walking beside a man whose wound was severe, but he refused to be left behind to take his chances with the Rebel surgeons. He was wounded in the head and arm, with his arm hanging in a limp fashion as a broken limb from a tree may hang in its final days before dropping off. He had a grayish tint to his face and his eyes seemed to be fixed on the landscape ahead as he struggled to find a pace to keep moving.

After a while he turned his head and said to me, "It was a good fight, wasn't it?"

I didn't know what to say to him. I didn't think it was a good fight—we were the ones pulling back, but in his mind he only remembered the actual battle and not the results.

"Yep, it was a doosey," I responded.

The shadows of his face were deepening and his tight lips seemed to be holding in check the moan he desperately wanted to let out.

"Yep, they kept comin' and comin' and comin'; they wanted a good fight this day."

As we continued our march we came across Frank Jones and he walked on the other side of this soldier. The blood was seeping through the wraps on his arm.

"Don't let the flies get to that, or they'll have a feast," Frank said to him.

But the soldier didn't say anything and continued his slow walk. Finally, he looked up and said, "Boys, you know what I'm afraid of? I'm afraid I'll fall down and them damned Artillery wagons will just roll over me. If I do, will you boys just drag me off the road?"

We both told him we would. After about 15 minutes through, he changed his actions and started to walk more briskly and direct. His eyes were focused on something in his mind and he walked with all the determination of a man with a special goal. There was a turn in the road ahead, but he kept going straight through a field, when Frank and I tried to stop him, he threw up his good arm and said, "Leave me be, just leave me be." We followed him until he reached the base of a big oak, where he sat down. He was at his rendezvous. No words were spoken, but within a short moment his chest began to heave and his limbs flogged about furiously. We went to him, but he yelled out, "Leave me be! Leave me be!" and with that, his body stiffened as if his soul was trying to escape the tattered and destroyed shell of human bondage and pass on into a more serene place. Finally, his mouth gave way to his last breath in this world and he lay under the oak in a most peaceful looking condition.

We took his personals and gave them to an officer we came upon, explaining his location. Frank and I looked at each other when we returned back to the road.

"Frank, I didn't even know his name," I said.

"It doesn't matter now; he is in a better place."

Finally, at about 3:00 in the afternoon we arrived at Harrison's Landing. We fell to the ground in total exhaustion, only bothering to take a few drinks of water and falling fast asleep under the nearest tree. Upon awakening after a few hours, the Army seemed to begin swelling quickly at this location and in a state of confusion. Soldiers were straggling in, looking for the location of their regiments; many were wounded having wrapped their wounds in pieces of clothing they ripped off of their uniforms.

The new base camp for our Army was located about 25 miles east of Richmond along the Williamsburg road and the northern bank of the James River. The center of the camp was located at the Berkeley Plantation. The ground here was exceedingly rich and fertile. The banks of the river sloped gradually and this continued into the water's bottom. In order to afford landing places for vessels, long wooden piers or wharfs have to be built.

After eating our first hot meal in three days, the six of us united once again took a walk around the perimeter. Our camp seemed to extend for about five miles entrenched in a small valley surrounded by hills on which our forces have been heavily fortified. If the enemy knew our location and the terrain surrounding it, they would see at once that a siege upon our camp would prove fruitless.

The large Berkeley mansion, two smaller buildings as well as several Negro huts were all occupied as hospitals. The owners and their slaves removed their portable personal belongings in April and May, but left all of their rich carpets and elegant furniture. It had rained heavily here a night or two ago and the rich carpets in every room were covered with a thick layer of the sacred soil. Upon these once elegant, but now muddied carpets, our wounded officers and soldiers are lying closely crowded together. Two of the rooms downstairs are used for amputations, and in this department of surgery, the surgeons have been busy continuously.

For the want of space, the sick and those slightly wounded are made to go outside the house, as there was only enough room inside for the severely wounded. There were a great number of sailing vessels and steamers out in the river being fitted to receive the sick and wounded and move them to more comfortable quarters.

The next few weeks we spent on ambulance duty, picket duty, and skirmish duty. There were a number of shirkers in our camp who were always sick or feeling poorly, therefore, they were given the duty of digging trenches to keep the sanitation disposal as clean as possible. But this was to no avail. Within three weeks of our encampment here, over 50 percent of the men had diarrhea, and malaria was making it's rounds as the mosquitoes were swarming everywhere in the stagnant heat of July and August along this godforsaken river. Men were getting the shakes on a daily basis; the hospital could no longer hold the number of men reporting daily. Then in early August typhoid began to hit the camp. Men with high fevers were walking about jabbering and muttering insanities until they lay down and died in their ragged, dirty uniforms. We called it swamp fever and every day we were forced to carry their dead bodies to the muffled drums beating out the dead march, it was sickening to our soul to see this unnecessary end to such brave men.

We stopped drinking any water that was not thoroughly boiled by one of the six of us. If we didn't have good water, we would throw our money together and find a sutler from which to buy whiskey. Franklin Higbe was the only one allowed to cook our meat; we trusted he knew what he was doing. Too many other soldiers' in the other camps passed around the cooking duties to those who didn't know how to cook and many of the men ended up with the inners. By the end of July, sickness had gotten so bad that half the Army was down. If the Rebels ever wanted a victory to probably end the war, they should attack now, as we didn't have the strength to resist.

The longer we stayed in this camp, the worse the conditions were. Food was getting scarce as our only replacements came via vessels off the river. There were never any fresh vegetables. We had an ample supply of hardtack, which was nothing more than flour, water and salt. Over time, this cracker would be so hard it would actually break your teeth when trying to bite it off and you had to be careful of the weevils laying their eggs inside the cracker.

Lemuel once remarked, "I think I need to beat this cracker with my musket butt to make it eatable."

Then our good friend and cook Franklin Higbe came up with an idea. He took our hardtack crackers and placed them in a canvas bag and began pounding the bag and their contents on the side of a log with a club until they became powder. He then added a little wheat flour he had obtained from a sutler, added some boiled water and rolled it into dough. He rolled the dough on a cracker-box lid like pie dough, we added some pieces of dried apples we picked up and he wrapped it in a cloth, boiled it for an hour and we ate heartily that night, thanks to Franklin.

Our meat ration, when it was available, was usually salt pork or "sowbelly" and we sometimes had to take the live worms out of it before cooking. Franklin usually boiled it on forked sticks. When we did get beef, it was usually fresh killed or pickled. Pickled was a like eating pure salt and fresh killed meat had to be cooked thoroughly. One day we drew meat and Frank Jones said it was so full of skippers it could move on its own. A lot of the time fresh meat was filled with maggots by the time it got down to our level.

By mid August sickness was becoming an epidemic while we were waiting on the Rebels to attack us. We felt McClelland was trying to decide what to do by playing politics with our lives. Finally, he got his answer from the President: "Withdraw all your troops to the defense of Washington."

What we as soldiers did not know was that a great plan had been laid out for all of our Armies under McClelland to meet up and join with Pope's Army of Virginia creating a 180,000-man force that could once again lay siege upon Richmond. What our leaders did not know was General Lee had already made the decision to risk the possible sacrifice of Richmond in return for the capture of Washington; the confederate capital could easily be moved, but that would not be the case for the Union. Lee had already begun to move his Army northwest towards central Maryland a week before we began to leave Harrison's Landing. Washington, which was being guarded by Pope's Army of Virginia of approximately 63,000 men now were awaiting the return of our army to join up with them near Manassas, Virginia.

A rebel cavalry raid on Pope's headquarters at Catlett Station the night of August 22nd captured the General's tent, dress coat, $350,000 in cash and most importantly—his dispatch book. The details of the plan to link up our armies and march to Richmond were confirmed with this book to General Lee. The Confederate Army of 60,000 would be no match for these forces if they were allowed to connect. His response was to order General Stonewall Jackson to immediately attack Pope in trying to stop the linkage of the two armies. General Longstreet was ordered to bring his Army to Jackson's assistance.

I believe all our men in all the armies felt relieved to be leaving such a horrid place as Harrison's Landing. The disheartenment we faced in our regiment was further fueled by the fact we would have to be the last Corp to leave. The 5th Corp left Newport News on the 20th, the third left Yorktown on the 21st, the 6th left Ft. Monroe (Aquia Creek) on the 23rd and finally we, in the 2nd, left on the 26th. The only information we received was that we were returning to Washington; we felt totally demoralized.

Upon our disembarking the sailing vessel, we were ordered to form up quickly and began a forced march towards Manassas Junction to assist in the fight there. However, by the time we arrived on the 30th we were too late; General Pope had been decisively defeated and had been driven back to Bull Run with over 4,000 men captured and 14,000 casualties. The confederate Army had already abandoned the area once our armies began to arrive, but the damage had been done and we suffered yet another humiliating loss.

We now moved back to our camp in Washington; however, we would only be here a few days before starting the next march to the next battleground. Time did not allow most of us to write to our homefolk, but we did receive some long awaited mail. The small amount of rest we received here was well deserved no matter how short it turned out to be. It has been almost a year now since we boarded that train in Randolph, but it seems like ten. I yearn to see home and friends again—especially Emma. Lemuel and Franklin are also very homesick; we need to get a furlough soon as our morale is already low. Just as some of us were about to put in for a leave, the orders came to prepare to leave camp on the next march.

CHAPTER 5
The Maryland Campaign

It was reported that the Confederate Army had invaded Maryland and was on its way to Chambersburg, Pennsylvania and Frederick, Maryland. Lee was a smart General; he knew the Northern Army had just suffered two major defeats and our morale would be low. He also needed to re-supply his Army and the untouched farms of the North would yield plenty towards that scale during the harvest time of the year. He also knew he didn't have to defeat the Northern Army militarily: he merely needed to make the northern populace and government unwilling to continue the fight. With Congressional elections approaching in November he believed that an invading Army playing havoc inside the North could tip the balance of Congress to the Democratic Party, forcing Lincoln to negotiate an end to the war.

It was now September 4, and Lee split his Army into four parts. The main Army had crossed the Maryland line from Leesburg and now was occupying Frederick Maryland. He ordered Longstreet to Boonsboro and then to Hagerstown, Maryland. Stonewall Jackson was ordered to seize the Union arsenal at Harpers Ferry. This left J.E.B. Stuart and D.H. Hill to defend Lee's rear at South Mountain. By splitting his Army, he cut off the supply line to the Union soldiers holding Winchester and Martinsburg and they were abandoned without a shot being fired. McClelland, being the cautious person he was, requested Harpers Ferry be abandoned and the garrison attached to his Army, but his request was refused. The populace reaction to this invasion on northern soil was to cause near panic in cities as far north as Philadelphia. The President pushed McClelland to go and deal with Lee immediately.

McClelland gathered up our 87,000-man Army and started to move westward in an ever slow lethargic pursuit. On September 13th we arrived at Frederick Maryland, only to find that the Confederates had abandoned the town and escaped through the gaps at South Mountain. Lemuel and I were placed on guard duty just outside the town to the southern end. We were joking around with each other trying to figure out why anyone would ever call these little hills west of Frederick, mountains; if they want to see some a real mountain; they needed to go to Randolph.

As we were talking and walking, Lemuel pointed down to what looked like a piece of paper wrapping tied around something. He picked it up and began to holler, three perfectly good cigars were inside. It was as if he had found a gold mine. Of course, being good friends and all, he offered to give me one of the cigars, for which I certainly thanked him. As we stood there lighting up our rich find, I started to look at the paper in which these cigars were wrapped. There written on top said "Special order 191," the order read about the Rebel Army's plan to split into four parts with the goals to disrupt the Union supply line in Harrisburg and attack Baltimore or Washington from two angles.

As I read this, I told Lemuel, "We have got to get this to General McClelland right away. You stay here and I will go take this to the sergeant."

Well, Lemuel and I were pretty proud of ourselves and when we returned from our time on guard duty we told everyone who would listen and we were quite the heroes for a short time. But after about 12 hours, we were still in Frederick and nothing was happening. We heard that Harpers Ferry was under siege directly to our south and we thought for sure we would head that way immediately, but we didn't. Then about 18 hours after we found the cigars, we were ordered to move out towards South Mountain in pursuit of General Lee. McClelland now knew that the entire Confederate Army was divided; he should attack the main body before they are allowed to consolidate back together again. However, Lee also knew his order had been compromised through a Confederate sympathizer that learned of McClelland's movement towards South Mountain and quickly ordered all of his Army back to the town of Sharpsburg.

Our Army moved out and our 2nd corp was again towards the rear of the march. There were three gaps to go through and the next day there were pitched battles fought for the possession of these passes. By mid-afternoon, General Franklin was able to break through Crampton's gap, but the other two held on for another two hours. We didn't see any action today, as we were too far in the rear and the roads through the gap were too narrow to move many troops at any one time, but by midnight, we had cleared the peak of the mountain and were in heavy pursuit. At about 2:00 in the morning we were ordered to halt and make our camp. We had no idea where we were except we had passed through the Gap at South Mountain and were moving into the small town of Boonsboro Maryland.

The next morning, September 15th, was a beautiful day; the sun was shining and produced a most comfortable amount of rays, a cool breeze was all about us and we were feeling that today would be the day we would get revenge on the humiliating defeats of the past. We left Boonsboro towards Sharpsburg where Lee lay straight ahead in front of our entire six corps. Jackson was still laying siege to Harpers Ferry and Longstreet was still en-route from Hagerstown; all we had to do was attack and the Confederacy would be no more. As we arrived later in the afternoon, we went into camp rather than spend the rest of the day in moving our armies into positions of attack and making preparations for battle. We heard that Jackson had captured Harpers Ferry this day. He positioned himself on the high hills surrounding the town and bombarded it into submission. With no place to retreat to, Colonel Miles surrendered his 12,000 soldiers to the Confederates. I thought to myself, if we had only attacked Lee today, Jackson would have been forced to come here to his defense and Harpers Ferry would still have been under our control.

The next day also was spent positioning our armies for an attack, while many of us were having conversations about why we were waiting. Jackson was now heading this way for sure and Longstreet had to be arriving soon too. It made no sense to us as to why General McClelland was waiting to attack. But the 16th came and went also with little to no activity other then a few advance skirmishers firing their guns every once in awhile. Then, at about 6:00 in the morning of the 17th, we were ordered to form up; finally the dance was about to begin. At 6:30 General Hooker attacked the left side of the Confederate Army from the woods to the right of the Dunker Church and the Hagerstown pike. The battle would go on until mid-morning.

At 9:30 in the morning, our regiment was combined with the 61st New York to form a small brigade, under the command of Col. Francis Barlow's brigade, which also included the 5th New Hampshire, the 7th New York and the 81st Pennsylvania regiments. We were placed on the far left of this line and held in reserve behind Meager's brigade. At about 9:45 in the morning, Meager's brigade started out from the right of Roulette's house advancing forward up a hill through an open field. As they continue their march towards the crest of the hill they were met with a heavy musket fire from the left and in front of Roulette's house. However, the brigade continued its advance even as many of its numbers were dropping under a continuous heavy musketry fire. As Meager's brigade advanced about half way up the hill, we were given the order to "forward march."

The musket fire was heavily intense as it passed through. It was like listening to a swarm of bees as they go past the ears. Meager's brigade finally reached the crest of the hill at about half strength, when they looked over the hill, they were facing thousands of the enemy entrenched in a sunken farm road with good cover about 50 rods away. They continued to fire upon the sunken road and a severe and well sustained musketry contest ensued; however, Meager's men were running out of ammunition and were severely reduced in numbers.

Our line had now advanced forward and joined in a line directly to the left of the 63rd Irish Brigade, and we continued to advance to just below the crest of the hill behind Meager's brigade, which was taking horrific losses. Within minutes, Meager's brigade had broken due to both the heavy fire and low ammunition. As they turned and went through our ranks towards the rear, I saw their faces. One young lad was so much in tears and shaking, his eyes were wide and his flight could not be stopped by man or beast. A sergeant passed near me who was shot through his face cheeks. His jaw hung dangling from his face disclosing the wide cavern of his mouth in a pulsing mass of blood and teeth. He was making an attempt to cry out as he ran zig-zagging in earnest to find someone to relieve his suffering. We were all now thoroughly terrified and death's image was all around us. We were still able to immediately move forward, but as soon as our heads crested the hill a barrage of fire came at us with such fury that I thought Almighty God had unleashed his vengeance against us. Franklin Higbe was hit immediately. I turned to him as he screamed out, but he motioned for me to go forward as he grabbed his arm and headed for the rear. I peeked at his wound as he turned to depart and his lower right arm seemed to be just hanging on to his elbow ever so slightly, it was just dangling in the air and the right side of his pants was covered in blood.

I immediately fired and hit the ground, reloaded, then unloaded another ball down upon the sunken road as quickly as possible. I didn't take any time to look about; I just concentrated with all my might on what it was I was doing. All the regiments were told by our officers to concentrate our aim on the center of their line. Directly behind the sunken road and in the middle of the confederate line was an orchard and to their right was a corn field. Both the orchard and the cornfield sloped downward towards the sunken road. In the orchard were pieces of artillery releasing their might against us as well.

After about an hour of heavy exchanges and our continued concentration to their center, their line finally began to break and men came out of the sunken road leaving all their possessions in retreat running through the orchard and the corn field. With this action, the Irish

Brigade began to move towards the opening in the center, but was repulsed by the continued firing from the far left of the enemy's line in the sunken road. Col. Barlow, now seeing the situation stopped the Irish Brigade's charge, immediately ordered the 61st and 64th regiments to align and make an oblique right turn towards the sunken road, thus placing us in a position of firing down upon the far left side of the sunken road. We quickly accomplished this task thus taking the enemies attention away from the Irish Brigade and after about five minutes of intense enfilading fire upon this enemy, we were told to stop.

Colonel Barlow announced, "If any of the enemy wanted to surrender, they should do so now or forever hold to the consequences."

About 300 men threw down their guns and surrendered to us along with two stands of colors. What a joyous moment this was and our cheers were loud and long. But the joy was short-lived as the left side of Col. Barlow's brigade was again moving forward now through the cornfield and to the right side of our company the Irish Brigade was also moving forward over what seemed like thousands of bodies lying in the sunken road. After securing and sending the prisoners to the rear, we realigned our lines and began going through the cornfield with the rest of the brigade. The enemy had regrouped over a slight hill in the cornfield and was throwing musketry at us; Albert Marsh went down when a bullet ripped through his leg. The confederate cannons located in the orchard behind the sunken road had now turned and were firing into us. Col. Barlow was hit within the groin area and General Richardson, severely wounded, had also been carried off the field. General Hancock had come up to assume command. Our brigade continued to advance against the rebels who were making a stand at the end of the cornfield, but our persistence prevailed and we drove them back behind the Piper house.

At this time, we were given orders to stop our advance and to hold this position. General Hancock had requisitioned artillery to his aid, but none were available. The Irish Brigade along with other regiments moved forward also, forcing the departure of the Rebel artillery from the orchard behind the sunken road. We held this position for the remaining part of the afternoon and were reinforced later in the afternoon with artillery from Kirby's battery. We remained here until evening, placing pickets out in front and receiving fire from the Confederate's sharpshooters. We were able to re-supply our ammunition during the night and by morning we were ready to go forward. During the night General Hancock received orders from General McClelland not to engage the enemy in an offensive manner as he was awaiting more reinforcements before continuing.

Henry Morgan and I were placed on picket duty together during the early morning hours of the 18th. We were posted some 100 yards from the Piper house below a small hill. We were very careful in raising our heads to look around as sharpshooters and rebel pickets were well posted in and around the Piper house. There seemed to be little sounds of major engagements around us. Sharpshooters were firing all day long and some musketry volleys could be heard in the distance, but no cannonade.

Then all of a sudden Henry said to me, "There's a flag of truce out there." I looked out but could not see one.

"Are you sure?"

"Yes, I saw it being waved on the end of a musket in the window of the house."

Henry, being of a single mind, immediately tied his nose rag to the end of his musket and raised it in the air. A response was heard from the rebel pickets, Henry and a rebel soldier conversed back and forth about the wounded not being collected for over 30 hours now and it being a shame as so many men could be saved. Finally, the rebel said General Pryor will speak only to our General Meager. Henry stated he would carry the message back to his commander. Henry left our picket and headed back through the corn field to speak directly with General Hancock. As he left, he was just full of himself as if he was brokering an end to the war.

Henry spoke to General Hancock and he immediately called General Meager forward to order him to meet and ascertain his wishes. General Meager, who knew personally of General Pryor, agreed to meet with him. General Meager mounted his horse and slowly moved out to the top of a hill where our pickets were placed just behind the ridge. A short time later, General Pryor proceeded out on his horse and the two men converged about half way between the two picket lines. After a few short minutes of conversation, the two Generals turned and rode back to their respective sides.

As General Meager passed our picket, he nodded and said, "Boys, keep a sharp eye out from this moment forward."

I learned later that Confederate General Pryor was under the impression we wanted a truce to recover our wounded and dead and when General Meager informed him that most of the wounded and dead were of his side and we had made no such request, General Pryor informed General Meager he had no authority to make such a request and the meeting was over. Well, Henry's big day as a battle broker ended. He continued to state that he saw a flag of truce in the window, but no one actually believed him at the time. However, the next day I was to agree with him as the rebel tactics would prove him to be right. In the meantime, as the Generals retired back to their positions, the sharpshooters continued their firing and it was returned in kind by us on the pickets, but without Henry—he was taken off picket duty and returned to our company camp.

About a half hour later, around 6:00 in the evening, another flag of truce was waved. This time it was waved in the open, and by an officer. General Meager was once again sent out to meet the bearer, who proved to be a lieutenant colonel. He stated the flag was intended to cover the operations of collecting the wounded and burying the dead, as he understood a truce was negotiated for that purpose previously. General Meager, being somewhat perturbed, informed the officer that he was mistaken and no truce existed, he turned and left the meeting.

In a few minutes, the hostilities recommenced. Subsequently, a number of the enemy appeared in the corn field directly in front of our picket—apparently for the purpose of collecting the dead, five of whom approached our picket where three of their companions lay dead. We immediately jumped forward and captured them. At that moment several shots were fired by their sharpshooters and two of our men on picket went down. The three of us remaining were able to deliver the five prisoners back to our lines without suffering any further injury. Our picket was replaced with six new men and we spent the night in the same camp position as previous.

The rest of the night was relatively quiet, except for a few sharpshooters letting a few rounds fly. The next morning, September 18th, we no longer faced a live enemy. All we could see were tens of thousands dead and wounded soldiers laying about in masses. The confederates had retreated during the previous day and night and left enough sharpshooters and diversionary tactics to once again slip our noose. It was a great victory, but our lack of pursuit of a defeated Army to end this godforsaken war made the victory feel like a defeat. The sunken road, filled with thousands of dead men and dead horses laying on top of themselves was a sight no man should ever see, for it will stay with him the remainder of his days on this Earth.

As soon as was feasibly possible, Lemuel and I made our way to locate our friends Franklin Higbe and Albert Marsh. We went back to the Roulette house, which now was a hospital, but they were not there. It would seem to be an impossibility to find them right now as the number of wounded lying around the outside of this house was in the hundreds. Arms, feet and legs were piled high outside the window of the operating room and the screams of the patient having his limb amputated was unbearable. Being unsuccessful at this time, we turned and went back to what was left of our company to learn of the fate of the rest of our comrades.

We found that our regiment had lost 40 men in our fight at the sunken road, 8 men were killed and 32 wounded. Of the 8 men killed, one was Spencer Earle, from Randolph. Eight of the 40 wounded were also from Randolph and from the original 43 who boarded the train on September 7th of the previous year. We are now down to 25 men. Our regiment is dwindling in size also; we have now lost 212 men since we left Camp Elmira.

The following morning General Fitzjohn Porter's 5th Corp pushed across the river at Boteler's Ford and attacked the Confederate rear guard at Shepherdstown. General Fitz Porter now ordered two divisions to cross the Potomac and establish a bridgehead. One division that pushed across was the 118th Pennsylvania who was with us at the corn field the previous day. However, General Pendleton, who was commanding the rear guard, contacted General A. P. Hill who led his division in a counter attack from the heights of Shepherdstown. The attack was devastating, inflicting 269 casualties and nearly annihilating the poor Pennsylvania division. That would mark the end of the pursuit of a defeated enemy by General McClelland.

The next few days, the two corps who were not involved with the fight, but held in reserve, were brought up to remove the wounded and bury the dead. During these few days of rest, we were in search of our friends, Franklin Higbe and Albert Marsh. On the second day of the search we decided to split up into pairs to continue our quest. Frank Jones and Henry Morgan would travel north along the Hagerstown pike and Lemuel Owen and I would travel east towards Boonsboro. We would stop at all hospitals and camps along the way asking about our friends.

Lemuel and I were about half way to Boonsboro at a little town called Keedysville. The road to the town veered off the right about 100 yards to a main street that ran perpendicular with the Boonsboro road. There was a spring running thru the town with houses on both sides of the main street. Each large house was occupied in some capacity as either a hospital or convalescing home for the many wounded soldiers. It was here by chance as we wandered through the town that we heard that famous sound: "Hey James boy!" As we turned, there he stood with his big round face staring at us. The lower half of his right arm was missing and bandaged with what looked like a large stump with clumps of dried blood on the end. But both Lemuel and I yelled his name in unison, so pleased were we to have finally found him.

Even through he was in a massive amount of pain, he was happy to see us and have us tell him how the rest of the battle went for our company. He also told us, he and others were waiting for ambulances to take them to a train station, as they were going home for a while. He said some were being discharged, but he refused it, saying he will return as soon as he is healed. I could understand how he would take that kind of stand; he was of strong character and truly believed in the purpose we were fighting for. I knew he would do as he actually said—he would return to finish the war in some particular manner. We spent pretty much the rest of the afternoon with him and when we asked about Albert, he had not seen or heard anything about where he might have been taken. We said our goodbyes to him about 4:00 and returned to our camp to hear what may have happened with Frank and Henry's search.

As we returned to camp, we were surprised to see Frank and Henry having a conversation with Albert. He had been released and allowed to return to light duty, as the bullet he received in his leg grazed his flesh and didn't hit any bone, just tore a little of his muscle. Other than being sore and having difficulty standing, he was glad to be back with us. He was another one who is strong-willed and truly believed in what we were doing.

CHAPTER 6
On to Fredericksburg

On September 22nd, just a few days following our fight at Antietam Creek, we were given orders to march to Harpers Ferry; Albert was given a pass to ride in the wagon. As we were preparing for our departure, word came to us that the President had issued a great proclamation that day. He proclaimed that effective January 1 of the following year; all slaves would be made free unless the southern states cease their rebellion. This proclamation created a tremendous amount of conversation among our men. It wasn't that anyone seemed to mind that slaves would be given their freedom, what was bothersome to most soldiers was slavery was not the reason we were fighting. We enlisted to stop the rebellion of the southern states from separating us as one nation, not necessarily to free the Black people. This conversation would continue for many days to come. Frank Jones, Albert Marsh and Franklin Higbe were those who agreed with the Proclamation and Henry Morgan and Lemuel Owen would disagree. I tried to remain neutral in all discussions and continued to remind everyone that there were only six of us left and we still had a job to do as the rebellion was still on—no matter if the Blacks were free or not.

One evening as we all sat around the camp fire, the discussion became quite heated about why we were now fighting this war.

Henry was quite upset and said "I don't give a damn what Lincoln did, he may have freed every goddamn blackie in the country; that is not why I came to fight this war."

"Your wrong," said Albert. "He only freed them in the states still rebelling and only by January unless the rebs quit fighting. He didn't touch the state of Kentucky."

"Well," said Henry, "It is still an insult to White men. No one will back him up."

Albert decided to just let the subject rest at that point. I could tell it was upsetting to both these boys as they were both headstrong on the subject.

I decided to seek out Frank Jones privately, to ask his opinion as I myself was now confused about why we were fighting this war. I found Frank inside his tent, kneeling and praying as he did most evenings before retiring. I waited a little while and then made a cough, which caused Frank to pause and look up.

"Frank, what do you make of this Proclamation that the President signed?" I asked.

"Well, a month ago, Mr. Lincoln was still meeting with some of the freed Negroes, urging them to search out a place in Central America to colonize. So the conclusion cannot be escaped. He has promulgated a war measure, nothing more."

"But I have read books about Washington and Jefferson and foul mouthed Old Hickory, which hint of the use of events to expand their powers in the Presidency itself and that could be the same here—with the deed performed and with the man, I just don't know."

"Yes, but he exempted any state that comes back to the Union by January. If he was a man seeking more power, why would he do that and allow those states that returned to keep their slaves?"

"No state will return to the Union; that's why it is a war measure."

I couldn't still understand the purpose and said, "Then what is the worth of the Proclamation, except to make the rebs madder and start an uprising that won't amount to much?"

"What is it worth?" exclaimed Frank raising his voice a might. "Let me tell you the worth of it: it is at the core of everything, however equivocated and compromised, it is the right thing to do. It creates, at last, a moral spine for this war. Now we fight for losing the shackles on fellow human beings."

I could tell not to take Frank any further on this subject, he was and has always been adamant about his reasons for fighting this war and it wasn't about stopping the rebellion.

I still hadn't changed my mind about why I was there. The adventure was out and now it was more out of a sense of duty to my country. Still, I was now more confused than ever and decided to take a walk in the moonlight to shake off the lingering revulsion from the sights of the campaign and this newest twist in the war's course. I then began to concentrate my thoughts on Emma as I walked along. Thinking of her seemed to place a quiet feeling in my mind, one that replaced war and death with peace and tranquility. As I returned to our tent to retire, I heard a melancholy bugle call that I had not heard before. It echoed through the bluffs surrounding the camp with a quietness of each note. I found out later that it was a new call saluting the fallen comrades of our many battles and it will be sounded each night to remind us never to forget them. The name of the call was labeled "Taps."

We were still part of the Right Grand Division under General Sumner and the 2nd Corp under General Couch. Our Division commander has changed to General Hancock because of the death of General Richardson at Antietam and our Brigade commander was now Colonel Van Schack, our regiment commander was still Lt. Colonel Enos Brooks. We were now the 1st Brigade and the Irish Brigade was the 2nd under General Meager.

The rebels were still in control of Harpers Ferry as we prepared to advance towards them; however, by the time of our arrival, they had retreated back to Jackson's base in Winchester. We made our camp and prepared to stay in Harpers Ferry for a while as McClellan was staying at Antietam until his Army reorganized and supplies were brought up. Just after making camp, the five of us applied for furloughs to go home for the first time since we left a year ago. Fortunately, three of us were granted leave until the middle of October, Albert Marsh, Lemuel Owen and me. We left on a train from Harpers Ferry going to Baltimore on September 24th.

As the train rolled into the old station outside of Randolph, I felt a sense of security once again as seeing the sites that I could only remember for the last year was swelling me with pride and envy of the tranquility. The town looked the same as it did when we left; the storefronts had not changed, but the people did not seem as joyous to our return as they were at our departure. I imagined that would be due to the number of boys who died or were severely wounded and were brought home in a horrible state. I looked for someone I might know when I got off the train, but could not find anyone. Lemuel had his family there as he got off the train, because he'd written and told them he was coming home. Albert had his sister there also in a carriage and he was going to drop me off at our farm on the way to his home. I didn't say anything to anyone about coming home, as I wanted to make it a surprise.

As I dismounted from the carriage at our lane and said goodbye to Albert and his sister, I looked around the old farm. How different it looked to me now. The house and barn seemed much smaller than they did when I left. The old oak tree in front of our wooden frame house seemed to be withering in the early fall weather. No one was around, so I went onto the front porch, which was now showing signs of needing repairs, and opened the door. The kitchen was to the left and the parlor was to the right. There standing over the wood cook stove laboring with her food as hard as ever, was Ma. She hadn't heard me enter and was intensely concentrating on her duties in front; her hair seemed grayer than I remembered and was neatly braided and rolled around her head.

"Hello Ma," I said.

She turned and dropped the ladle from her weathered hand and screamed out loud, "My God, he has brought you home to us!" With that, she ran over and put her arms around me as I don't think she has ever done in the past. She held on to me for dear life, all the while weeping tears of joy.

After a few minutes she let go and started yelling for Pa and my brothers and sisters who were in fields behind the barn digging up the last of the potato crop for storage during the winter. They all came a running—even Pa with his bum leg. It was truly a happy moment and my decision to make it a surprise was a good one as we talked for the rest of the day and evening. The next morning I asked Pa if I could use the carriage for a while to visit with Emma. Of course he said, "Take it all day if you wish." On the way over to her parent's farm, I wondered what I might say to her about all I have seen this past year. I also wondered if I had changed in her mind after being away for so long. As I pulled into their long farm lane, these thoughts left my mind and I focused on trying to see her among the people outside doing their chores.

As I pulled up to the farm house, Emma's brother came up to me and shook my hand, saying all the pleasantries one would say to someone who has been away so long. I quickly acknowledged his graciousness and ask if Emma was about. He told me she was helping to clean out the barn stalls from the morning milking. I immediately began to make my way towards the barn about 30 rods behind the house. Emma's family was large, five brothers and four sisters, and Emma was just about in the front of the pack in age. As I approached the barnyard, I noticed someone with a fork load of manure coming out of one of the stall doors, so I just hung my arms over the yard gate and stared at the door until she came out again.

As she threw the manure into the back of an old wagon, I yelled out, "That job would be fitting more to a boy rather than someone as pretty as you."

She turned towards me, gently put her fork against the side of the barn and said, "If there were enough boys left around here, I wouldn't have to do this."

She than came over to me and gave me one of the biggest kisses I think I have ever gotten. She was as happy to see me as I was to see her; all those thoughts I had previously entertained were now gone from my mind forever.

We spent the rest of the day together; I helped her with her daily chores and we talked about everything. I spoke to her somewhat of the trials of a soldier's life; I left out the battle parts and the scars that have been imbedded in my mind. It was just wonderful being home and in a peaceful environment with family and friends. Emma told me she has been volunteering to help at the local convalescing homes near Randolph for those soldiers returning home in a wounded state. I could not have been more proud of her than at that moment, for she was kind by natural impulse and her charities were regulated by such a good sense they would never demoralize any recipient.

For the next few weeks, I would visit with family and friends and on Sunday, we would have many folks over to our place for dinner and conversations. I would help Pa run the farm during the day and spend the evening with my beloved Emma. The time seemed to pass so quickly. The next thing I knew it was October 15th and I knew we had to bid farewell once again to all the folks who we loved so dearly. Departure this time was much harder than before. This time the folks surrounding Randolph had seen and felt the results of war and were not in the same celebratory frame of mind to see us off. Concern and fear filled their faces, as we boarded the train back to Baltimore. There were no bands playing or speeches being made; instead hankies were filled with tears, and there were shouts of instructions for us to be safe and careful. It was a painful departure, but one which we all knew had to be done.

Before we left, Emma and I laid out some plans for marriage when my enlistment was up and I was able to return home for good. We didn't tell anyone; I insisted it wouldn't be prudent. My fear was of returning in a box and not giving Emma the ability to advance her opportunities of marriage for some time while she would be mourning over a dead fiancé. Reluctantly, she agreed to not mention a word to anyone. This was not a point of compromise—I have seen too much of how death can happen to a soldier so quickly.

While on the train back to our duty post at Harpers Ferry, Lemuel told me of his desire to continue to stay home with his wife and family as they were in need of his support to continue on living, but he was more bothered by the oath he gave and came to the conclusion his word as a person wouldn't be worth spat if he didn't follow through with his commitment. I could tell he was having a hard time leaving his family as I was leaving my Emma. But if there was to be peace, it couldn't be left up to others to provide it; we made our commitment and we had to stick to it.

Upon return to Harpers Ferry, we found our company had just returned from a reconnaissance trip to Charlestown and were settling back into a daily camp routine. The main Army itself was still in camp at Antietam, not having moved one inch since the battle there. We heard the President was making a trip to see General McClellan and might come to Harpers Ferry to catch the train back to Washington. We were all relatively excited about the possibly of seeing and hearing from the President. A few weeks went by and it turned into November 1st. The autumn skies here were filled with a brisk cool wind and the mountains surrounding this town were of the most beautiful array of colors. Mother Nature chose to bring this all together where two great rivers meet to form a picture as pretty as only God could create.

General McClellan was starting to lose favor with some of the soldiers these days; his lack of aggressiveness at Antietam and Fair Oaks made for constant talk around the camp fires. His trying to mix politics and war was starting to fuel rumors amongst the men. We heard that the President went to meet with him at his home when he was in Washington in October, but the General, upon arriving at home chose to go to bed rather than meet with our President. These kind of discourtesies and insubordination towards our President was fueling a discontent among our men. We then learned that the President had just finished his meeting with General McClellan and was en-route to Harpers Ferry to board a train and speak to the soldiers.

The five of us now together gathered along the side of a steep hill near the armory to listen to what our President had to say. It wasn't a very long talk, but what he had to say made a big impact on our minds.

The President said, "I have just met with General McClellan and said to him that since he has chosen not to use the Army to pursue the enemy, I would like to borrow it for awhile. With that I relieved him of his command and suggested he go home to New Jersey for a short rest and await instructions from me."

We all could tell that the President was somewhat perturbed with the General and his inability to be an offensive General and I think he was trying to relay to us his frustrations and let us know he wasn't going to tolerate it any further. The new General in command of the Army now was General Ambrose Burnside and it wouldn't be long before he would have us engaged once more.

General Burnside had a great plan for the capture of Richmond by using a diversionary tactic. His plan was to concentrate the Army near Warrenton, Virginia, forming a movement to attack Culpepper or Gordonsville, then he would rapidly shift his Army southeast and cross the Rappahannock River to Fredericksburg hoping Lee would sit still not knowing what Burnside's intentions were. Then the Army would make a rapid movement against Richmond along the three railroad lines leading into Richmond. Jackson was still in Winchester and would take some time to arrive to assist Lee's Army. Burnside began assembling a supply base at Falmouth, near Fredericksburg. To make this plan work, six pontoon bridges would have to be built and sent to the front ready for quick assembly. This would enable his Army to cross the Rappahannock quickly to Fredericksburg, which was being guarded by only about 500 troops and then we would load onto trains to Richmond before Lee's Army could react.

We were ordered to break our camp at Harpers Ferry on November 15th and formed up for marching to Fredericksburg. On November 17th, our brigades were the first to arrive at Falmouth, Virginia, to re-supply for the crossing to Fredericksburg. But because of administrative bungling, the bridges had not yet arrived. General

Sumner strongly urged an immediate crossing of the river to scatter the token Confederate force in the town and occupy the commanding heights to the west of the town. But his request was denied as Burnside became worried that the increasing autumn rains would make the fording points unusable, leaving Sumner cut off and destroyed. He ordered us to wait in Falmouth.

By November 21st, Longstreet's Corps had arrived near Fredericksburg, and Jackson's was following rapidly, Lee noticed how slow Burnside's Army was moving and decided to consolidate his Army at Fredericksburg. On November 25th, the first pontoon bridges started to arrive—much too late to enable the Army to cross the river without opposition. However, Burnside still felt he had an opportunity, because he was facing only half of Lee's Army, not yet dug in, and if he acted quickly, he might be able to attack Longstreet and defeat him before Jackson was present.

Once again, this opportunity failed to materialize as the last of the six pontoon bridges did not arrive until the end of November. By that time Longstreet was dug in above the town at a place called Marye's Heights and Jackson had arrived. Now, that the surprise was gone, Burnside was thinking the confederate Army was spread out and an attack in the center would break their line. He also had an enormous amount of artillery to cover any possible attack from the heights above Fredericksburg.

On December 11th engineers began to assemble six pontoon bridges: two north of the town center, three on the southern end of town and one in between. These men came under punishing sniper fire. In order to slow this fire, landing parties were sent across the river in boats to establish a beachhead and roust the snipers. At the same time the artillery let lose an enormous amount of shells on the town and ridges to the west.

Our 2nd Corp was to cross with Hookers Corp on the two pontoon bridges north of the town center. We began to cross the bridges on the 12th, two men abreast as quickly as possible careful not to sway so much as to fall in the rapidly flowing river. Once on the other side we were stopped and bivouacked here during the night. On the morning of the 13th we were organized into our attack order. A line of the enemy was now about a mile long. Our entire Army faced the daunting task of defeating an enemy that was very high up and well dug in.

This same morning, a heavy fog covered the entire area; the divisions at the south end of town moved forward around 8:30. We could hear the commencement of fire, but had no idea to what extent the fighting was. This was to be Burnside's main attacking point and we felt rather fortunate not to be in the division first called out, as the fog was very thick.

At 11:00 in the morning we received orders to move out. We were to move through the town of Fredericksburg towards the Marye's Heights position where Longstreet was well entrenched behind a stone wall. We were ordered to move in brigade order leaving 200 steps between brigades. The first to go up this long steep hill of at least

600 yards was General French's two brigades, followed by the Irish Brigade and then ours. As we marched double quick through the streets of Fredericksburg, the shelling and sniper fire was so intense it was dropping men and officers every few seconds.

By 3:30 in the afternoon French's brigade was repulsed with extremely heavy losses—and now it was our turn. General Hancock sent the order for General Meager's Irish Brigade to move forward from their location along the street in Fredericksburg. Upon arriving at the entrance to the field of battle, I noticed the difficulty that awaited us. The stone wall was at least several hundred yards away from our location on Hanover Street. In order for an attack line to be formed, all the brigades had to march out into the open field by flank while under immense fire from above. They then must turn left and begin to advance forward up a steep grade of some several hundred yards towards the stone wall. General French's first brigade entered the field under a most murderous fire of artillery and musketry, losing some 10 percent before they made their left turn to go forward.

They began their advance as the next brigade marched by the flank to a position behind them. After about 200 steps, the next brigade started their advance. The first brigade had the unsavory duty of cutting down fences as they made their advance forward. The first brigade was very much destroyed in the first hour of fighting. Each brigade behind them was able to draw a little closer to the wall before having to forego their efforts or be destroyed.

The Irish Brigade in front of us made their march out, made the turn and started moving forward. Now it was our turn to apply our talents.

My God, I thought, we are going to be cut to pieces. Even though these were my thoughts, we were hardened fighters now and having been through battles before felt that God would have his pleasure of either saving us through this day or making a place for us by his side. As we turned to march forward behind the Irish Brigade, a load of grape found its mark to our left line and at least four men fell. The march, with our flags raised high was one of looking ahead, moving quickly and trying not to stumble over the enormous amount of men lying on the ground in front of us. What was left of French's brigade was now out of ammunition and was rapidly making its departure back through our ranks as we were going forward. We were now within about 200 yards of the wall; the Irish Brigade was within 100 yards and was taking a terrible number of casualties.

All of a sudden, we heard the cry of Colonel Pat Kelly for the Irish Brigade to prepare to charge and within seconds, he yelled charge and what was left of this brigade began to make a rapid assault towards the wall. Seeing this bravery, we became excited and our Colonel Brooks followed immediately with his orders to follow the assault right behind the Irish Brigade with our own "Charge." We quickly fixed bayonets and began running forward. I could barely see the wall through the field of smoke about 50 yards in front, when all of a sudden I screamed out in agony; a burning sensation brought my body down to an immediate halt. I was hit in my left upper leg.

I went down like a rock, the searing pain felt as if a hot iron had pierced my body. Trying to keep my senses about me as bullets were flying just over my head, I quickly turned my body around and began to use my arms to pull my body back down the hill. I advanced only about 50 yards when my arms gave out. I saw two dead soldiers lying just to my right, parallel with the wall. As quickly as I could I pulled myself behind one of these brave men and tried to move one body over the other as best I could to give me cover from the onslaught of fire coming down. I was able to roll one man on his side propping him up against the second man. I then tore some pieces of shirt off the dead man and tied it around my wound. I didn't know the severity of my injury; just the constant burning pain was all I felt.

I remained there for an hour or so as men ran passed me; they were quickly trying to get back to the rear and safety. It was now about 6:00 in the evening and all our brigades had fallen back to a line just beyond the town. The wall was never breached and the battle was now an artillery fight; however, sharpshooters were posted at the wall and taking aim at anything that moved in the field of battle. I didn't move an inch until darkness had completely fallen; I was afraid to even look around me, so I kept my head on the ground and snuggled as close as possible to the bloody cool bodies in front of me.

The night was fairly clear, giving the sharpshooters good targets for taking shots on any movement they may see. I did eventually lift my head and look around. I noticed other wounded soldiers that had done as I had and were using the dead as protection. The air had now turned very cold and so were the boys with whom I was sharing the ground. We could not communicate between the wounded as I heard someone speak about 20 yards to my right and a barrage of shots rang out in that direction. I never heard another sound the rest of that night. My thoughts were of being captured. If the confederates poised to counter-attack in the morning, there was nothing I could do but surrender myself to their mercy. If we recommenced our attack in the morning, the odds were good that a ball or grape shot would find me as a target and I would enter the next life quickly.

Morning came and there was no offensive attack on our part and no counter offense on the part of the Confederates. I just continued to lie there, then in the early afternoon, I heard soldiers coming onto the field and no shots were being fired. I later found out the General Burnside had given up his attack and asked General Lee for a truce to remove the dead and wounded and it was promptly given. I was able to finally move without fear of being shot. I sat up and looked at my position. I was about 100 yards from the wall where I could easily see rebels staring at me. Then, suddenly one of their soldiers raised his hand at me and waved, but I wasn't sure what to do. I thought perhaps they knew I was there and didn't fire during the night; I assumed that was the purpose behind such a gesture, so I waved back.

My friends finally arrived to help me down on a stretcher and I was certainly happy to see their sorry-looking faces. I noticed as they carried me down the hill in a litter the number of thousands of wounded men being loaded into the hospital wagons. It was an absolute bloodbath here. Six divisions separated into brigades made this attempt at the wall; there were 6–8,000 casualties as a result. Our regiment lost 3 of their 27 officers and 105 of the 408 men who started. Colonel Miles was severely wounded and his loss had a devastating effect on our men.

As I was being loaded onto one of the wagons to be hauled away to a makeshift field hospital at our old camp in Falmouth, I said farewell to my friends and comrades who came to my assistance and told them not to worry, and that I would return. I was traveling in a four wheel ambulance that was built with shelves, or compartments. The most severely wounded would lay in the bottom shelf and the lesser wounded on the top shelves. We were compelled to ride for over two hours while receiving a terrible jolting from the road. We had four horses, but were twice swamped on the road, causing we wounded to have to depart the vehicle until the wheels would turn again.

As I lay waiting to be re-loaded back into the ambulance, I took special notice of the other wounded soldiers with whom I rode. Two of these men were wounded in the face, one of them having his nose completely severed; the other having a fragment of his jaw knocked out. A third had received a ball behind his knee, and his whole body appeared to have been paralyzed. Two were wounded in the shoulders, and the sixth was shot in the breast, and was believed to be injured inwardly, as he spat blood and suffered most horribly with the pain of imminent death.

The ride with these men through the wooded countryside was traumatic in itself. Throughout the still of the day their screams would be frightening to all wild game and insects and even the birds in the trees. One soldier sang out in a shrill, fierce, fiendish ballad in an interval to obtain relief, only to fall, in a sudden relapse, into prayers and curses. They called aloud for water to quench their insatiable thirst, but the wagon just kept moving at an ever slow pace.

As we arrived at Falmouth, I noticed especially that all the mansions, houses, barns, wagon sheds, hen coops, Negro cabins and cow houses had been turned into makeshift hospitals. As we passed some of these places looking for one with enough room for us to be disposed of, I noticed inside the doorways that the floors were littered with corn shucks and fodder. There lying on the floors were the wounded men, who were maimed and dying. A few slightly wounded men stood at the windows, relating incidents of the battle, but at the doors stood sentries with crossed muskets to keep out idlers and gossips.

We finally stopped at a barn converted to a hospital. I was unloaded first and taken inside to be placed on the floor in line with others who were awaiting the surgeon's message. The shrieks and shouts inside this large room were beyond description. Men with their arms in slings walked restlessly back and forth, smarting with fever. In many wounds the balls still remained, and the discoloration of the flesh from being swollen unnaturally had begun. The worst were the soldiers who were shot in the belly, their constant spasmodic cry for "help me" or "my God, have mercy" only ceased as they moved into an unconscious and lethargic state. I shuddered as I thought of the poor soldier lying next to me, who was told by the assistant surgeon mercifully that he could not live. I will never forget the longing look in his eyes reaching out in a desperate plea for someone on whom to call to reverse those words.

As I lay there for about two hours, I was visited by a male nurse who gave me some opium and liquor to help with the pain. He told me it would be quite a while before I would be attended to as amputees would come first, followed by wounds such as mine, he informed me. Anyone who was shot in the head, neck, chest or abdomen should make peace with his maker for there was little that could be done for them.

Finally, after about 12 hours, I was taken in to see the surgeon. As we entered the operating room, I noticed an eerie scene, as there was a pile of arms, legs and fingers at least five feet tall in the corner. I was immediately given quinine with opium and in a short period could barely see this fellow who was dressed in a blood- and pus-stained coat. He held his lancet in his mouth while working on me. He prodded in the hole where the ball had entered and exclaimed it had exited cleanly, with no bones shattered. My wounds were seared shut with a hot iron, packed with moist cotton and bandaged with wet bandages. I was told to keep the bandages wet and I would be given small doses of whiskey and quinine to help with the pain of healing. The next day I was given a set of crutches and told I would be moved to a convalescent home in Washington for awhile. The trip there would be hard and painful for all those wounded men who were lucky enough to be selected to go. The ride was by wagons over very rough roads for three consecutive days.

Upon arrival at the convalescent home I found it to be a terrible place to be quartered. The severely wounded who made it this far after falling ill to disease or wounded in battle found they were left to God's intentions, as the only medicine they received was morphine. The men who were sick with disease were separated from the men who were wounded. The diseased soldier was a most dismal looking man, barely made of pure skin and bone; some could not sleep or even lie down. They seemed almost to be out of their minds—constantly mumbling, twitching, and with fever. I was glad not to be quartered with them.

Every day was the same routine; breakfast was at 8:00; if you didn't eat your breakfast you would get no lunch as food was not to be wasted on those who choose not to eat. I was able to get about some on my crutches and I visited the General Store on the grounds and was able to enlighten my taste buds with a few pieces of hard candy. My wound seemed to be healing naturally, as I did not notice any signs of infection or swelling and the pus was forming up quite nicely. I spent quite a lot of time catching up on my writings to home and to my friends back at camp. Even through I am grateful to be alive and given a rest, I miss not having friends in the camp to speak with. I needed to recover as quickly as possible.

As I sat there, my thoughts moved me through the progression of time over the last 18 months. I remembered how contrite my life was before I enlisted, how I wondered what was on the other side of those beautiful New York Mountains, how much I miss Emma and my family. I then turned my thoughts to my experiences of the Army. It started out as a great fun adventure with a free ticket to see the outside world that has turned into one of the most debilitating rides of the mind one could ever have. I have lain in the smell of the stench of someone's extremities. I have watched another person lie dying from the diseases caused by man's inability to enforce cleanliness. I have seen young men's bodies blown apart by the destruction force of the enemy. Oh how I need to leave this place and put these thoughts behind me.

By the end of January 1863, my wound had healed enough that I was able to walk without the need of crutches. The doctors at the hospital said I could return to my company and I was elated to be able to leave this place. The Army has now been based in Falmouth for the winter so the trip to locate my company did not take long and I was anxious to hear what has happened, as the Army now has a new commander named General Joseph Hooker. Burnside had been relieved after another ill-fated attempt to capture Richmond through the so called "Mud March."

Upon arrival at camp, I was able to locate my friends and they were certainly glad to see me. We exchanged warm greetings and shared a good cooked meal prepared by one-armed Franklin Higbe who had returned to our company as a cook while I was healing. As my friends knew of my keeping track of the original 43 men who left Randolph together, they told me we were now down to just 21.

They began to tell me the story of the ill-conceived "Mud March" they experienced a few weeks before. Burnside continued to look for weakness in Lee's line at Fredericksburg. Lee had dug in for the winter with a line of over 25 miles that was thinly stretched. Burnside was still reeling from his own folly in direct assault in December and still determined to attack by deception. He ordered preparations as though we were preparing for crossing the river once again at scattered points, miles apart. New roads were cut, pontoons brought up, guns dug in, companies were marched back and forth and the cavalry was sent to demonstrate under enemy eyes.

His real plan was to cross the river some ten miles north of Fredericksburg, this sweeping maneuver would put him on the left flank of Lee's Army and he could roll it up. As our Army moved westward, all the while carrying on an elaborate deception downstream, Lee started to strengthen his left side of his line late and Burnside had the advantage. On January 21st, the plan called for a division to cross at the same point as before in the middle of Fredericksburg distracting the rebel Army while the main Army would cross over the river at the same time using five pontoon bridges ten miles north.

But fate was to once again befall this General. The night of the January 20th it rained so long that all the roads were shocking. At the appointed hour to begin the deception, not one pontoon bridge was in place, some 150 pieces of artillery were stuck in the mud requiring triple teams of horses and mules to pull them out. The rain was still coming down all day as our Army struggled to move the pontoon bridges and artillery. Burnside refused to give up; he ordered food forward for two more days.

The following morning he authorized a whiskey ration for everyone. But the rain kept on. It was an indescribable chaos of pontoons, wagons, and artillery encumbered along the road down to the river. Horses and mules dropped down dead, exhausted with the effort to move their loads through the hideous medium. At least 150 dead animals were counted in the course of a morning's ride—many of them buried in the liquid muck. Now, the General's problem was no longer how to move to attack, but how to retrieve his Army from the elements.

From across the river, the taunts of Rebels sang out. Every Yankee there remembered the sting of the broad shouts put out by Lees watching men. "Yanks, if you can't place your pontoons, we will send help," was one expression heard by Frank Shannon. Albert Marsh told me of a story of how low the morale of our Army had been reduced. The first night of movement during this great rain, a captain of the 3rd New York artillery, with whom our company was helping to move the cannon, sought out the sergeant of the guard. He found the sergeant drunk and proceeded to reprimand him. The sergeant ran for his pistol, and like a madman took out after the captain, who hid behind a tree, then stepped out as the sergeant passed by and cut the sergeant down with his sword.

"It is a sad time when we start attacking our own soldiers while leaving the enemy to slide so easily," Albert said sadly. Everyone now thinks Burnside was just full of bad luck and was happy to see him relieved and Hooker to take command.

Our Army spent the winter camped between Fredericksburg and Falmouth Virginia. We built our wood hut shelters and insulated them with the abundance of mud and straw available. The morale of the Army has to be at an all time low. It seems about 100 men a day are leaving their posts and going home, disgusted over many things—losing battles due to poor leadership is just one item, not being paid for over six months gripes us more. Not having replacement uniforms or enough food has put the strain too high on many of the men to continue on.

When we visited other campfires at night, the talk was always of criticism of the government, officers and of quitting the service. The only thing that held many soldiers back from just starting to walk home was the regulation that stated deserters would be shot. Dissatisfaction became so great that soldiers were shooting off their extremities in order to get a discharge. This mood was very evident with Henry Morgan. It was evident he still felt a grudge against the leaders of our Army over the "white flag" incident at Antietam. He was expecting an apology for him being made a fool of when pulled off of picket duty. The continued poor leadership only convinced him more that our Army is doomed to disaster.

During this time Henry became very vocal on the President's policy and his desire to compromise with the enemy; he was trying to convince the rest of us that we should join him and just lay down our arms and go home. Finally, after listening to his comments for quite some time, Albert Marsh, who was now a sergeant, just told him straight away and didn't mince words, "Either shut up or move out." Henry never said another word to us from then on out about the war, but neither did he speak any more to Albert. The tension in the air between us friends was an added strain on our now long relationship.

General Hooker took a personal interest in rebuilding the morale of his Army. His dynamic leadership quickly manifested itself by demanding the improvement of food rations, making sure the soldiers' pay was caught up and paid regularly, replacing worn out uniforms and equipment and he renewed the ceremonies, drill, and tightening of discipline.

To help his endeavor, the President instituted the conscription act. This was the drafting of soldiers into the Army to replace the more than 200,000 men who were already killed, wounded or died from disease. This had a little effect to boost the morale of the existing soldier, but was a detriment to men who didn't have the spirit to join. However, to satisfy those of means who were not interested in getting their hands bloody, but desired to relish in the rewards of victory, they were allowed to pay $300 to the Government and provide a substitute person in their place. This was hard for the average everyday man to swallow. It was as if a rich man can buy his way out of his patriotic duty, but the poor man who was working to support his family had to go to war. The people of New York City were so enraged that a protest riot took place in the streets for days, leaving scores killed until a brigade from the Army was able to bring order.

While General Hooker brought us back into the fold of a better, more equipped Army; the discipline side was a more difficult project. Insubordination of our enlisted men towards those of superior ranking was an issue that the General would no longer tolerate. A private in our company, being a contemptuous sort, lashed out at our company captain when assigned extra duty for his refusal to drill.

"You are goddamned trash! You think you can do just as you goddamn please because you are an officer! I'll be goddamned if I will perform the duty—I'll see you in hell before I will or I'll shoot everyone of you sons of bitches!"

The private was then arrested and sent to the guard house. We never saw him again, but we heard he was court martialed and spent the rest of his enlistment in a prison near Washington; forfeited all his pay and received a dishonorable discharge.

General Hooker was very serious about the disciplinary treatments for not following orders, or for insubordination, but the most serious I ever saw were the poor soldiers who feel asleep on guard duty or showed cowardice during battle.

On an early February morning, we were told to form in brigade order at 10:00 in the morning. As our brigade was formed, we were marched to an open field where another brigade had also been formed. I had heard of Private William Scott being given the death sentence for being found fast asleep while on guard duty, but I was not aware we would be forced to witness such an execution. As we gathered, I saw a young boy of about 18 years being marched out to a lonely tree in the middle of a large field. The look upon his face was one of complete despair, as the captain escorted him to the location where a horse had been placed; the captain began reading the charges to which he was found guilty by court martial. When the reading of the charge had been completed, he was placed upon the horse; a complete silence was felt throughout both brigades who stood watching the fate of this young man. It was at this point in time when a messenger on horseback rapidly burst through the lines towards the captain. The captain read the document, turned to the brigades and announced, "By decree of the President of the United States, Private William Scott is hereby pardoned from the charges brought against him." Both brigades erupted into cheers, but were quick to be quieted by our officers. The young man was let down off the horse and allowed to return to his company. I think he shall never be lax in his duties again. I don't know if the President actually pardoned him or not, but the effect of this display had a major impact on the rest of us and the possible consequences of failure to do our duty.

In early March, Henry Morgan got a furlough to go to Philadelphia to visit his folks. We all felt it was a little odd he would want to go see them as it was they who sent him to his Aunt and Uncle to live in Randolph. In any event, the day he left he came around and said his goodbyes to each of us, except Albert. It was the odd way in which he talked that we all felt he would never return. He would rather become a deserter than continue to be part of a war in which he did not believe.

"James," Henry said, "I want you to know you have been a fine friend to me, better than some of the others who I left Randolph with and I won't forget your kindness."

"Henry, why are you talking so? It sounds as if we will never see you again; you are only going home for a few weeks."

Henry turned with his belongings in his hands and said, "Just remember, there are people that will say anything to manipulate the use of events to their own desires, even if it means sacrificing thousands of human beings in the process."

With that he turned and walked off to leave and I knew then without doubt that he would never return.

It didn't bother most of us when he left—the tension had been high between him and the inner circle since Albert issued those sharp words to him previously. He knew we would never take his side against our country and leaders.

As he moved farther away in his walk through the camp, he turned and called to me, "Take good care of yourself, James; don't let the rebels finish the job they started in Fredericksburg," and with that he was gone. We were never to see or hear of him again. When his furlough was up and he didn't answer at muster, he was officially marked as a deserter. Since he wasn't really from Randolph, there would be no shame for him as he was not returning home to Randolph, he simply could go to Philadelphia, state his enlistment was up, and go on about his business losing himself in a large city.

The months of March and April were ones in which we became an organized Army again; our pay was caught up, we received new uniforms and shoes, our equipment was replaced if needed, the food improved substantially, and new recruits were joining our company daily. We would drill every day and all the while the new recruits, having very little, if any training, would ask us veterans questions about battles and fights until they were blue in the face. Most of the time, we didn't mind their inquisitive nature, but there were times when the remembrance was difficult to recall without becoming emotional.

CHAPTER 7
Chancellorsville

March proved to be a warmer month than usual, and along with all the improvements that General Hooker made, the Army has started to regain its morale back. It has now been reorganized and we were under General Couch's command in the II Corp, 1st Division under General Hancock, 4th Brigade under Colonel John Brooke and our regiment commander, Colonel Daniel Bingham.

General Hooker has now laid a great plan to attack General Lee and end this war. He would leave Sedgwick and Reynolds Corps at Fredericksburg to once again attack the heights, but he would march 60,000 soldiers starting on April 26th, 15 miles north and west, we will cross the river at Kelly's Ford on the 28th, and swing left to attack Lee's left flank at Fredericksburg and roll him up. Our II Corps would march on April 28th to Bank's Fords some five miles northwest; General Sickles was crossing his Corp at United States Ford some seven miles northwest; and all 118,000 of us would be in position to simultaneously attack Lee at his front and his left flank by May 1st. Pontoon bridges would be sent forward to prepare for the crossing of the Rappahannock River.

As luck would have it, J.E.B. Stuart's Cavalry, while out on patrol, saw the movement of some of our pontoon bridges going west. He reported that information to General Lee who countered by having Stuart's Cavalry move parallel with the pontoon bridges. They then captured some union advance pickets protecting the pontoon movements to Lee's left around the Chancellor house, but the oddity was realized when they discovered the men captured came from three different Union Corps. Lee, now knowing the move of the Union Army, ordered 80 percent of his Army to move on a force march to Chancellorsville, leaving 20 percent to slow the move of the forces crossing at Fredericksburg.

At 2:00 in the morning of April 27th we rose on orders to break our camp, which was located just below the Lacy House, and prepared to march. We marched until daybreak and halted at headquarters where we were formed into the 4th Brigade. We then began marching again towards Banks Ford where we arrived at 11:00 in the morning. We were told to encamp there for the night. We were near some pine woods to the right of the main road. Two hundred of our regiment was detailed to help build a corduroy road through the woods to Banks Ford. Lemuel, Frank and I were detailed while Albert and Franklin Jones were left to do latrine duty at camp.

This was tough duty after just marching 12 hours. We had to cut the trees down, trim them and lay them cross ways on the newly formed road so the wagons could bounce their way along. By morning, we were relieved of our duty by the rest of the regiment so we could rest a bit. But it wasn't to be for long, for at about 1 o'clock in the afternoon we heard the bugle call to break camp and prepare to march once more. It was just our regiment who was leaving though; we were to march forward to Hamet's crossroads and hold that position while the rest of the brigade passed and then follow the rear of the wagon and ambulance train. Again, our duty was strenuous as the heavy hospital wagons were constantly being stuck in the mud and causing us great energy and delays in catching up to the brigade and getting into camp. We finally arrived at midnight, totally exhausted.

It was now April 30th, and we began marching towards U. S. Ford at 8:30am. We arrived at noon, mustered up again after resting a bit and marched until 6:00pm, when we reached the Rappahannock River at a location with a steep and rocky bluff. We then crossed the river on pontoon bridges and marched until 10:00pm along a main road to Chancellorsville. We then camped next to the Pennsylvania 53rd Regiment with our front to the east.

It is now May 1st and we broke camp around noon, with orders to march our Brigade about one mile to the top of hill along a road running northeasterly. We were the leading regiment. As we approached the hill, General Hancock ordered our regiment across the road and to deploy one half of us as skirmishers and to keep the remainder in reserve with our right connecting with the 61st New York. As we marched, Franklin Jones was in front of me. He had been promoted to sergeant after Antietam, so he had a number of us for which he was responsible. Franklin isn't a bad sort of fellow, though his high-pitched voice sometimes doesn't reflect the distinction of being a sergeant. Sometimes, when he shouts out an order for us to follow, it reminds me of my Ma who would scream out that supper's on the table. But his determination on the battlefield more than made up for his voice.

It was now 1:00pm and the five of us are part of the advanced skirmishers and we have gone a considerable distance into the woods. Shelling from Stuart's Cavalry has begun and is well over our heads and nearer to our reserve. It didn't take very long for our reserve to move forward, closer to us to avoid those shells. We had now advanced to the edge of the woods, halted and waited until the rest of the regiment caught up to us. An open field lay ahead of us and we could see that action had already started with another brigade.

We began to form up our brigade into a line of battle. Our line was fronting the northeast and left of the 145th Pennsylvania brigade and to the right of the 27th Connecticut. We were sent out again as skirmishers, but it was dusk and we could just barely see the enemy who was in great force to our front. The shelling began as it became darker, but there was no attack. It was 8:00pm and we, as skirmishers, were told to build breastworks and dig trenches, which we did and finished at midnight.

At 3:00 in the morning, an officer came out to us and told us to go back with the greatest of secrecy to the regiment. Upon arrival with the regiment, we were told to march quietly back to the brick house along the same road we marched on earlier in the day. We were then told to build breastworks and trenches facing northeasterly. We quickly began moving as quietly as could be expected, and completed our breastworks and trenches by 7:00 in the morning. We were really exhausted, barely having any sleep for two days, but our thoughts were not of our muscles, but more of whether or not we would live through this upcoming fight.

We lay behind our breastworks all morning, trying to catch some sleep while keeping one eye open. Then about noon time, shelling began to fall in on us. Two men were wounded with grapeshot and we huddled tight in our trenches, but no advance was made. The day was long and the wait seemed to be forever tiresome. It became dusk once more; this time General Hancock ordered our entire regiment to be deployed as skirmishers to the woods some 600 yards in front of the brigade's breastworks. About midnight we were ordered to move out of the woods, where we were somewhat protected, and march down a road to a point where rifle pits had been dug by a previous occupying tenant. We lay in the pits all night; they were deep ones, some as much as four feet deep. We could hear the enemy clearly in the calm clear night, they were moving troops just in front of us, the sounds of wood being chopped, orders going out and owl signals being tossed about were as clear as if they were standing next to us.

Finally, the sun started to rise and as soon as there was enough light to see clearly, we heard the orders of our enemy officers, "Prepare to advance." It was at this time I felt a weakness again in my legs; it felt as if I was doomed to a hangman's noose. The courage to fight like this doesn't come from inside one's person, but from the surrounding friends who help each other prepare for what may be someone's last day on this earth.

Out they came. The skirmishers first appeared in the horizon directly in front of us advancing with their ever present peculiar yell. After they'd advance about 50 yards, our officers yelled "Let them go boys," and a volley went out that sounded like a thunder cloud breaking open. They immediately stopped and fell and a continuous barrage of fire was thrown in both directions for about half an hour until they retired.

Roughly ten minutes later, the next attack began. This one was by a regular line of battle on our whole front, with closed ranks. Again, after about 50 yards we let loose on them, but this time they held their ground, continuing to advance on our position with the greatest of stubbornness. They drew to within five to six rods of our breastworks and we fought continuously for one hour before they retired in confusion. This gave way to cheers from our entire line even through we could plainly hear the chilling cries of the wounded enemy lying so close to our front. It was a short-lived glory to behold, because about 15 minutes later, they came at us again.

It was another line, but the formation was the same as previous. The difference was we were starting to expend our ammunition rapidly. An urgent message was sent to General Hancock for more ammunition; this time our men began to fall from the enemy getting so close and us with so few shots left. Finally, they broke again after about one hour. The cheers went up again, but not as lively this time. For now, the wounded cries from both sides were more overpowering in sound than our glory.

In another few minutes, the enemy showed again, this time they were in a double column and closed in mass. They were focused on making their charge directly to the middle of our line. There was no time for us to move men. Colonel Bingham ordered the right and left flanks of our lines to oblique their fire towards the center and to not fire until the signal was given. Our ammunition was just about exhausted; some men from the Pennsylvania 145th regiment was sent to help us and they were scattered, but shared their ammunition with us. The problem was their balls were too big for our barrels, so we had to use just the buckshot, which meant we had to be close. Bayonets were loaded and we were ready for the impending assault. They were making ground this time and were just about to climb the breastworks when, to our surprise, they rapidly fell back. They were so close to us that Charles Bingham from company G jumped out of his pit and captured six confederates.

With no ammunition to continue, we were finally relieved by the 27th Connecticut at 9:00am and filed to the rear for re-supply of ammunition. We stayed at the rear the rest of the day and ordered to set up our camp; we were happy for the break. We never knew why they cut off their attack, but we were all glad it happened.

It was now May 4th at 7:30 in the morning. We have been ordered to support Battery C, First Rhode Island Artillery a short distance down the road from where we were yesterday. We built breastworks and entrenchments by 11:30 in the morning while dodging fire from rebel sharpshooters. Other than that, it was a quiet day. The next morning, enemy skirmishers showed themselves to our left, but the Battery immediately began shelling them and they retired. About 4 o'clock we received orders to hold this hill at all costs even if the Battery retires. Within an hour of receiving these orders a violent storm erupted; it was one of the worst I have ever seen. The lightning bolts and thunder just over the top of us lasted for a good hour. Our trenches filled with water, our clothes were completely soaked and felt like we were hauling a ton of stone on our backs.

At dusk, the Battery was ordered to retire and us to fall in behind them, we marched back to the Rappahannock River at U. S. Ford and the Battery crossed over about 10:00 pm, we were then told to guard the rear until all batteries had crossed, then we were able to cross at about 3:00 am. We then marched the remaining of the night back to our original camp.

We learned the battle had been another loss as part of the rebel Army under General Stonewall Jackson had encircled our right flank and surprised over half of the brigades in a late evening attack on the first day. They had captured thousands of our soldiers forcing us to immediately pull back and go on the defense. Being unaware of these circumstances, we were no less disappointed again.

The following day, we learned we were to return to our original camp site near Falmouth, Virginia. This would be the end of our second campaign to capture the city of Richmond, and once again it ended in failure.

As soon as we returned to our base camp, the six of us asked for and received a 20-day pass to go home. We were all in need of a few weeks of rest. Franklin Jones had not been home since the day he left and God knows he was deserving of it.

The train trip home was very quiet this time, the thoughts of this war and the sad sights we have witnessed weighed heavily on all our hearts and minds. Our regiment started out in Elmira some 18 months ago with over 900 men; we now had about 200 left. Of the original 43 who started out on that train in Randolph, 19 of us were left. We had nothing but sad thoughts to think as we passed the night away looking wearily into the darkness of the night and listening to the constant clattering of the train as it moved over the tracks.

Upon arrival back in Randolph, we noticed the mood of the community was subdued. No one came out to greet us; many women were dressed in black either mourning their husbands, sons or close relatives who had ventured into another life where there were no wars and sadness to beset one's family so. When I arrived at home it was towards evening and the sun was just beginning to set. Ma and Pa were sitting quietly on the front porch and Pa rose to stand as the wagon approached the house. We exchanged greetings and I was more than happy when Ma offered to fix something for me to eat. I then noticed she had grown much grayer since my last visit and Pa seemed to be moving at a much slower pace with a slight stoop in his walk. There were more worry lines in their faces than had been there before and their eyes seem to be worn from the swelling of past tears that have flowed. The war had taken a toll on them as well; we had lost three of my cousins and two uncles—one on Pa's side of the family and one on Ma's. During my consumption of the fine vittles Ma made I was told that about every family in and around Randolph has suffered the lost of a loved one. The people's mood has changed from total support of the President to "when will he stop the killing?"

The following morning I rose early and hitched the wagon to start to head towards Emma's home. She knew I was coming home from the letters I had sent her, so I imagined in my mind she would be excited and would be expecting to see me. But to my dismay, upon arrival she was not home—she was at another farm in Cold Spring helping to tend to three wounded brothers who had been sent home. Her Ma told me the convalescing homes were filled and she had now been going from home to home when the wounded arrived and offering her services to help change the bandages and help feed the wounded. Some of the boys she was tending had severe wounds and didn't survive. This form of death had hardened her spirit to continue on her assistance with all her strength. I told her Ma that I understood and to please leave a message for her that I came to visit. I then turned and stepped up into the wagon and went home.

The next few days I spent helping Pa around the farm, thinking how good it would be to just stay here and get up at dawn when the rooster crows, work the fields, care for the animals and not speak or see anyone outside of my family for a long period of time. I yearned for the days of old and was thoroughly disgusted with myself for my earlier desires to leave such a beautiful area. But I knew I could never stay longer than my leave allowed as the bounty hunters would find me and I would be a disgrace to my family. It was a selfish thought anyway. How could I ever stay while my friends all returned to the hell and fury of battle again. I banished these thoughts from my mine.

On the third day a wagon pulled up to the house. It was Emma. She came to me immediately and said how sorry she was not to come sooner, but she was staying at a neighbor's farm overnight and didn't know I had arrived. I told her not to worry, her work was more important to those who have returned in such a deplorable manner.

We spent the rest of the day sitting by a brook under a large shade tree not far from the barn. I told her of the battles and the details of my wound and she told me of the returning sick and wounded. It was a time when both of us could release to each other our pent-up feelings of anger and frustration this war has caused. Was it so important to keep our Union together anymore and who cared if the slaves were free or not? I had never even seen a Black man before I enlisted, so why should I care if they are ever given their freedom? We both had seen the pain and suffering caused by the greed and determination of poor leaders and it has sickened us thoroughly. But alas, at the end of the evening we knew we could never tell anyone of what we said to each other. I must go on and finish my obligation, for it was my word and my signature that must be honored; if perhaps not my heart.

When Emma left, I felt as if part of me went with her that night. In her presence I felt a sense of relief and cleansing from the pain and suffering I had seen and experienced. There was no one else I could tell my inner thoughts to, for it would certainly show a sign of weakness that would not have been accepted by others whom I know so well. I slept well and content that night for the first time in many a month.

The time was near for us to return to our regiment in Falmouth. As reluctant as we were to leave our loved ones once again, we found the courage to say our farewells and boarded the train to take us back to the dungeons of hell. The ride back to Washington was as quiet and uneventful as it were coming home. We all knew too well what we were going back to and no one was willing to discuss the matter. We just sat in our seats and stared into the moonlight as the trains passed back through the silhouetted towns we have grown to know so well.

CHAPTER 8
Gettysburg

We arrived back in our camp in Falmouth the first week of June of 1863. There had been quite an amount of verbal activity going on. Rumor had spread that the Confederates were leaving the heights of Fredericksburg and were on the march to a place we know not where. Apparently, after the battle of nearby Chancellorsville, General Lee had to re-organize his Army because of his loss of General Stonewall Jackson. We were not aware that his Army was suffering from a food shortage of any great proportion.

General Hooker, in the meantime, was regrouping and rebuilding his ranks of men so the Union Army could make another attempt at capturing Richmond. On or about June 8th, it was reported by our cavalry that some regiments of the rebel Army was seen marching towards Culpepper. General Hooker sent a reconnaissance force across the Rappahannock on the 9th and it immediately encountered heavy resistance at Brandy Station. This convinced him the main rebel force was still between Fredericksburg and Chancellorsville.

What General Hooker did not know was General Lee had started to execute his plan to invade the north and end the war. His plan consisted of three main goals. One goal was to move his Army into the rich fields of the Cumberland Valley of Pennsylvania where he would easily be able to obtain food and supplies for his troops that was no longer available in Virginia. The second goal was to entice the Union Army to follow him, thereby giving protection to the capital city of Richmond, as his Army could not withstand another major fight on their soil without food. The third goal was to destroy the supply and communications systems in Harrisburg, a major distribution center. Wreak havoc on northern towns until the people and politicians who have become increasingly despondent on the war will apply enough pressure on Lincoln to force an offer of settlement.

It is now June 13th and General Ewell was re-capturing the city of Winchester. We suffered yet another tremendous loss there with over 4,000 men being captured. After the battle of Winchester, General Hooker was convinced that Lee's Army was moving north. It was a matter of finding the location of the main Army, trying to anticipate what the enemy's plans were and to prepare a defense to stop them. Not having any knowledge of the location of the main Confederate Army forced the President to order General Hooker to proceed northward keeping his command between the Confederate Army and Washington. Today the 1st, 3rd, 5th and 11th Corps left to rendezvous at Manassas Junction. Tomorrow, June

14th, we will start to move our 2nd Corp with the 6th and 12th towards the same rendezvous point. Our Army of over 95,000 men is moving north and west; Lee's strategy was working.

The entire Confederate Army is now moving from Fredericksburg to Culpepper to Winchester to Martinsburg, across the Potomac and into Williamsport and Hagerstown Maryland. General Ewell and his II Corp, has orders to go through Chambersburg, Carlisle, and into Harrisburg, Pennsylvania. General A. P. Hill has orders to follow General Ewell and break off at Chambersburg with his 3rd Corp and move through Gettysburg and on to York, all the while protecting Ewell's right side and keeping the Union Army at bay while Ewell can perform his destruction of these towns and cities. General Longstreet with his 1st Corp will move along the east side of the Shenandoah Mountains until reaching the Potomac, then follow General A.P. Hill until he breaks off at Chambersburg; then Longstreet is to fall in behind General Ewell's Corp enroute to Harrisburg all the while protecting the supply line and the rear of the Army. General J.E.B. Stuart and his Cavalry had orders to protect the passes on the Shenandoah Mountains until the Army has passed, then to engage the Union Army when feasible on the east side of the Mountains through Pennsylvania.

We are marching about 15 miles today. It is a very slow march; we are stopping often until the Cavalry reports its results from their reconnaissance missions in search of the Confederate Army. The days are much longer now and much warmer. Our supply packs are filled and the load is heavy to carry. There isn't much talk in the ranks as we move along, I'm concerned about Lemuel—he hasn't said much at all since we left Randolph. His facial expressions are unreadable and his demeanor is lacking any emotion at all. He just stares forward as he walks, quietly keeping all his inner thoughts to himself. Tonight we will camp at Dumfries and await orders to move on to Manassas Junction.

Each day we go through the same routine and we continue to march yet another 15 miles listening to the canteens clambering against medal while the drummer boys beat the same set of taps over and over again. Everyone seems to feel a certain oddity about this march. It is as if there is a special cloud of uncertainty hanging over our heads as we move along. It is filled with evil and destruction, yet the cloud's fog is too thick for us to see the Devil, but we can feel his nearness, prying inside our heads as we remember our past battles and worry over our future ones. General Hooker has sent out his cavalry towards Harpers Ferry and Martinsburg to find any information on the location of the enemy. They returned with rumors of sightings of the enemy at Point of Rocks and Shepardstown, but no major force was found.

On June 17th we arrived at Fairfax Station. It is here we will stay for the night. Sixth Corp was moved to Germantown, Maryland after General Pleasanton's cavalry captured eight confederate officers at Aldie.

It is now June 19th and our cavalry still cannot locate the enemy's Army; all the passes over the mountains are well protected and our cavalry cannot break through. Our 2nd Corp was moved to Centreville. General Hooker believes Lee is planning to attack him over the Blue Ridge Mountains and capture Washington since he has not yet crossed the Potomac River.

General Hooker is becoming very worried about his command. He is demanding the President place local militia units under him, send him the marching units protecting Baltimore and Washington and let the new enlistments stay back to form a last line of defense.

It is now June 22nd and the President bends and gives General Hooker command of the 8th Corp protecting Baltimore and Washington and we continue on, a few miles at a time each day.

Now, it is June 24th and General Hooker has moved two Corps to Frederick Maryland. Three Corps, including our 2nd Corp is at Middletown, Maryland and one Corp is at Knoxville Junction. General Hooker is visiting Harper's Ferry where he finds 10,000 soldiers in defense on the Maryland Heights, but no enemy is to be found. He wants the President to allow him to add these men to his Army and abandon Harper's Ferry. He also is demanding the arrest of General Slough for not adding his militia men to his Army. He tells the President he does not seem to have the authority to win the battle through the politics of Washington. The Army is now stretched from Frederick, Maryland, to Harper's Ferry, Virginia.

June 27th, General Hooker offers his resignation to the President and it is accepted. On June 28th, General Meade assumes command of the Army of the Potomac. Reports are now coming in of Rebel forces marching through Hagerstown and into Chambersburg. Meade starts moving the Army north to Taneytown, Maryland. Each day we move another 15 miles north and each day General Meade is sent telegraph messages from the War Department of sightings of the Rebel Army well into Pennsylvania. General Meade now knows the Confederate Army is moving towards Harrisburg and immediately begins to bring his Army up.

It is now June 30th and our Army is marching cautiously towards Harrisburg through roads leading to Hanover and Gettysburg, Pennsylvania. Messages now report the Confederates are as far north as Carlisle, Pennsylvania. The cavalry has fought with J.E.B. Stuart on our armies right flank as he is making his way towards Carlisle from York. Our Army now had its positions at Emmettsburg on the left and Manchester on the right.

It is now July 1st, and General Buford has sent word back to General Reynolds of the 1st Corp. that his Cavalry unit has made a significant contact with a brigade size force at Gettysburg and is in need of immediate assistance as larger forces are moving down the road from Cashtown. General Reynolds and his 1st Corp immediately start to march towards Gettysburg and sent orders to General Buford to hold Gettysburg; they are but a few hours out. In the meantime, word is sent to General Meade, who orders General Reynolds to move his 1st Corp towards Gettysburg, and shortly thereafter, he ordered our Corp to start marching in the direction of Gettysburg. It is now with great anticipation that our regiment moves; we only have about 200 men left of the original force and all are battle weary, but the new recruits cannot be trusted as many have not yet been tested. We march with the greatest of zeal as if we couldn't wait to get there.

General Reynolds arrived around 10:00 in the morning and immediately ordered his advance division of the 1st Corp to deploy and attack the enemy coming down the Cashtown road. He then ordered General Howard's 11th Corp to advance to the northern part of town as quickly as possible. It was at this point a sharpshooter found his mark on General Reynolds body and immediately killed him as he sat in his saddle. First Corp now fell to the command of General Abner Doubleday who fell into line to support the heavy fighting against the Rebel forces coming into the town of Gettysburg from the Cashtown road. He also spread his men to the northern part of town to protect his flank.

General Howard arrived at about 11:30 and was now in command of the field. His 11th Corp, arriving quickly, fell into support for the 1st Corp, which by now was heavily engaged from both the western attack down the Cashtown road and from the northern attacks down the Harrisburg and York roads from Ewell's Army coming from Carlisle. The Rebels coming from the west and north with such a large mass of troops were more than our forces could cope with and by the time General Hancock arrived at about 4:00 pm General Howard had ordered both 1st and 11th Corp to fall back to Cemetery Ridge to the north and the Emmetsburg Road to the west and south of town.

General Hancock now took control of the field as ordered by General Meade. He immediately began positioning the arriving Corps into the high grounds. At about 7:00 pm General Meade arrived, approved General Hancock's positioning and extended his plan as troops arrived. The 11th Corp was placed on Cemetery Ridge, the 1st Corp to its right and the 12th Corp to the right of 1st Corp. To the left of the 11th Corp along the extended southerly portion of Cemetery Ridge was our 2nd Corp and to our left was General Sickles' 3rd Corp extending to Little Round Top. The 5th and 6th Corps were to be placed in reserve as they were not going to arrive until the next day after a 36-mile forced march. During this time of posting the location of Corps for a defensive battle, the enemy continued to attack on the northern part of our line around Culps Hill; however, our forces were very strong there and by dusk, the Rebels retired back to the town, which they now occupied.

We did not arrive until the early morning hours of July 2nd, and immediately we formed our line along Cemetery Ridge. Our Brigade was once again in the rear of the march and we were to be positioned with the 3rd Corp to our left. However, there was no 3rd Corp directly to our left, General Sickles had decided on his own to move his 3rd Corp about half a mile further in front of the Ridge passing through a wheat field; he formed a "U" line, with his pickets on the Emmitsburg Road. His left was touching the bottom of Little Round Top and his right line was angled back towards us, but with a large gaping hole of about 400 yards unprotected.

As we watched for enemy movements during the day, we were blessed with the arrival of General Meade passing our Regiment. He looked thoroughly worried and disgruntled. He asked Lemuel if he had seen any officers from the 3rd Corp and Lemuel replied he had not. The General then simply turned and continued on. Later, we were told he was looking for General Sickles to have him move his Corp back along the Ridge line with the rest of us. I would imagine he would be having a few choice words ready for him from the way he looked to us.

It is now about 3:00 pm and troops continue to arrive. The 5th and 6th Corp have been placed in reserve behind us and to our left flank. We can hear the drums of the enemy beat off in the distance, both to our front and left; we know full well they are planning an attack soon. We are preparing our defense by building short walls of stone found lying in abundance throughout this area. All the while, our thoughts begin to focus on the fight ahead and the remembrance of family and friends so far away. The sun remains ever so warm and the sweat is pouring off our brows as we hear fighting again from the northern part of our line near Culps Hill. It is now only a matter of minutes until the battle and our adrenaline begins to flow at a rapid pace. I am moving faster while not seeming to advance in any one direction.

It is now 4:00pm and we hear the large claps of what anyone else may call thunder, but we know it as grape and canister balls being thrown into General Sickles' line about a half mile in front of us and to our left. After about half an hour the sounds of musketry began and we knew it was time once again for the dance to begin. We then see General Meade to our left, riding quickly to our line asking to see General Hancock immediately. He informed General Hancock that General Sickles was under severe attack from the left woods against his line from Little Round Top to the Emmitsburg Road and is in great need of support to hold his position. He then ordered 5th Corp out of reserve with half the Corp forward to a position on Little Round Top and the other half to the aid of General Sickles' line.

General Hancock now ordered General Caldwell to move all his brigades downward and toward the wheat field to drive back the rebel attack. Our brigade was organized quickly and marched south towards Little Round Top; we then turned right and marched towards the Emittsburg Road With the Irish Brigade on our right. As we worked our way through thick woods we came upon a fierce fight in the middle of a wheat field. As soon as we broke from the woods, we were ordered to charge the field, which we did in earnest. As I was moving towards the action at the wheat field, I became somewhat cognizant of my feet and body moving at a rapid pace and my eyes staring to my left, then my right, looking for the first sign of someone taking aim at my body.

As we grew closer to the action, I noticed off to my left an accumulation of large boulders looking as though they were formed together as a fort. From this area I was able to see many Rebel soldiers firing upon our left flank. The ground was filled with dead and wounded men and not a strand of wheat was left standing. The screaming and fighting was of immense proportions with bayonets being thrust about for self preservation. The 3rd Corp was backing away from the force of the Rebel charge. However, upon our arrival with freshly loaded ammunition, the four companies of our brigade were able to inflict immediate harm to the driving force and it was stopped.

Colonel Brooks, our brigade commander along with Colonel Kelly of the Irish Brigade rallied us on to continue to push the rebels from the wheat field. We kept moving our feet forward, only stopping to stoop down on one knee to reload another cartridge, get up and move forward firing at our targets as we advanced. I believe the rebel's ammunition was at a low as they fell back from the wheat field into a wooded ravine giving them good protection from our open advance, but they kept on going, up the other side of the ravine, exiting the woods to our left. We pursued them until we reached the end of the woods at the top of the ravine. From here we could see clearly the EmmitsburgRroad and the open fields.

We waited at this point, trying to collect ourselves with our units as all the men were scattered throughout with little knowledge of where their units were. I could not find any of my friends, as I feel I must have moved to far to the left while advancing through the wheat field. Albert, Lemuel, and Franklin Jones were nowhere to be found. I began asking for the whereabouts of Company B when all of a sudden shouts rang out: "Here they come again." It was as if all of God's anger was upon us. The Rebels had regrouped and were coming at us hard with at least two brigades from the left. I began to fire at their charging line and was reloading when I heard someone shouting, "They're coming from the right also." I looked up and saw another brigade coming across the Emittsburg Road to our right.

We had not the forces to withstand this amount of pressure and it wasn't but a few minutes that we heard the bugle ordering us to retire and we began pulling back quickly, beyond the wheat field, towards our original line on the ridge. There were about 100 men I was with who continued to fire forward one last time before pulling back. As we did pull back in confusion, a number of us ran too far to the right as we tried to get through the thickness of the woods looking for the clearing from which we came. When we finally exited, we found ourselves surrounded by Rebel soldiers who had already captured the ground on our right. Our confusion in the woods just cost us our freedom and we now became the prisoners of a regiment of Alabama Rebels. For us to attempt to fight any further would have meant certain extinction from this world. We threw down our guns and stood there as a few of the

Rebels took charge of us and marched us off to their lines. They now seemed to have control of all the ground up to the base of Little Round Top, and we hoped and prayed they would not advance any further that day.

It is now 8:00 pm and in a matter of a few hours, I became the property of another human being, subject to his conditions and wishes. We were at once marched past the massive amount of Confederates encamped along seminary ridge. They were mostly a ragged-looking bunch, only about half of them had any shoes. The Alabama boys who captured us let us keep our blankets and all that we had—indeed except for our arms and equipment, of course. We were marched up the Cashtown Pike to the top of the mountain where we could no longer see what was going on at the field. Here we were turned over to guards who were in charge of the teamsters, shuttling supplies and ammunition to and from the main Confederate Army. We were told to camp ourselves under some of the trees for the night, and this we did without question. We were given some water, but no food.

The next morning we awoke to new experiences. Instead of the calls to which we had been accustomed, we were but passive beings, subject to the will of a conqueror. In the early part of the day, rations were issued to us for four days, consisting of 25 hard crackers and about two pounds of raw salt pork. They were from the provisions taken from Gettysburg and consequently we thought were of good quality. There were now around 200 of us and about noon we were told to line up and begin marching due west towards Chambersburg, with the teamsters hauling out their wounded and the dead that were recovered from the previous day.

By evening we were passing through Chambersburg. Folk were on the streets looking at us as we passed by with disbelief.

"How dare they take our young boys from us," stated one elderly woman who was standing by the road as we passed by. Young children and women were all we had seen along our route through Chambersburg, there were no young men about and I suspect it would be dangerous for them to show themselves if they were here. We bedded down along the road in a corn field this night. We were able to start a fire and boiled some of the salt pork we were given before the skies opened up with a downpour of rain. There was nothing we could do; even if a shelter was near, our captors would not relinquish any movement for us. After about an hour, the rains passed and we settled ourselves into the cradle of Mother Nature's wet arms.

About mid-way through the night we were awoken by our guards and ordered to prepare to march quickly. We were being organized when another Union soldier came up to me calling my name. "James" he said, I turned and was completely surprised to see my friend Lemuel staring at me with his still black carbon face and mud-covered uniform. I was glad to see him of course, but would have preferred the meeting to take place under different circumstances. He told me he had been captured at the foot of Little Round Top just as he was about to jump over a boulder and head into the woods. The Rebels who caught him dared him to take one more step as it was their thinking to not have to deal with any live prisoners. While it is not a desirous position to be in as a prisoner, with Lemuel along, it made the plight a little more bearable.

We began our march over the dark road towards Hagerstown. There seemed to be a sense of urgency among our guards, which confused us. We were marching along side the dead wagons. The wagons carrying the wounded never stopped to rest the night before as we did, they kept on moving back towards Virginia, so why were the guards so demanding of our continuing to march at such a rapid pace? We couldn't figure it out, but if anyone would show signs of fatigue, he would feel the pain of the pointed bayonet in his back and that would instantly make him come back to par with the group.

When we arrived in Hagerstown, we stopped for water—more for the horses than for us, but the village post-master came out among us, promising to mail letters for us. We soon loaded him down with as many short letters as we could write in such a short spell. I wrote to Emma along with a letter to my folks, not wanting them to worry so much about me, but to know I may not be writing to them for an unknown amount of time. After our short, but grateful rest, we started up again, marching until way after sunset when, upon arrival at the Potomac River we were allowed to rest a bit, fix a fire and cook more of the salt pork we were given. We were allowed to rest for about three hours and then we crossed the Potomac on pontoon bridges into the land of secessionism or the state of Virginia as we preferred to call it. Once inside their border, we were allowed to camp for the rest of the night. We fell in the same place where we stood for we had no more energy left to establish a bed of comfort.

The next morning, having rested peacefully during the night, we made some "crust coffee" from the water along the road side, and with some hard tack had a bearable breakfast. We were then allowed to go to a nearby brook and wash ourselves of the mud and grime we had accumulated over our bodies during the past four days. We then fell in for a march that lasted the remainder of the day until we reached a place called "Bunker Hill." It was at this place we would stay for a number of days. The location was rich in water as three streams ran within a quarter mile radius. We were made to place our camp just south of the corner church from the main road in an open field. Our hosts pitched their tents surrounding our encampment thereby securing our stay.

It was here the next day we saw the return of the entire Rebel Army from Pennsylvania—such a ragged looking bunch as I have ever seen. They looked as if they had been shot through the cannon themselves, many missing parts of their clothes, still covered with the black carbon faces and looking the worst of wear as if they had traveled non-stop for days at a time. We resorted to various expedients for amusement, trading between our boys and the Johnnies seemed to cause considerable merriment for both sides. But at the end of the day, we were still prisoners, without shelter and without enough food to satisfy our hunger.

We stayed in this encampment for about three days. One morning a rebel officer came up to one of our officers and announced that half of us would be moving out to the south and half to the east. We knew what the east meant, for it was the "Libby" prison located in Richmond. The reputation of that prison had already stood among us as one in which we would have no pleasure taking shelter. Not many of our soldiers who were fortunate enough to survive their stay rendered any compliments about their visit. It was as if the unknown seemed more inviting than the known destination. Lemuel and I stayed close together so as not to be separated when the division began. We were both listed with those who would be going south.

There were about 400 of us now at Bunker Hill; 200 of us were formed up and started marching to Winchester where we were put on trains and shipped further south and deeper towards the center of this spider's web. The train had stopped, we were told, somewhere in North Carolina, and we disembarked. The guards told us we were to march towards the town of Tarboro, a distance of about 22 miles. We marched for 12 miles before nightfall, taking shelter near some pine woods. It rained some, but the pine trees along with using our blankets as a tent protected us as best they could. The next morning we marched the remaining ten miles before reaching the town. We were counted as we proceeded to pass through an immense crowd consisting of both sexes and all classes.

They had congregated for no other purpose, but to examine and criticize us poor unfortunates.

Lemuel and I, along with everyone else, were nearly starved by now and we were bartering away clothing, gold rings—whatever could be exchanged for a bit of something to eat. Five dollars in northern money would buy a piece of corn bread, baked with little or no salt and about the size of your palm. The citizens of this town were perfect extortionists and robbers; we gave up whatever we had for the food they were willing to give us. The next day our group was again broken up: two-thirds of the men were going to Goldsboro and the rest of us were slated to go on to Charleston.

We boarded a train from Tarboro; we were placed in a boxcar and made to stand for the entire duration of the trip. We stood so close together as to not to be able to sit even if we desired to do so. By night we longed for a little sleep, to lose ourselves in grateful unconsciousness for a little while. As soon as night fell, the officer of the guard ordered the doors closed and we passed a most miserable night, nearly smothering each other and pressed almost out of all shape. The next morning, we arrived and drew rations of three small crackers and a little scrap of bacon to subsist on. It was evident our hosts did not intend for us to suffer from overeating. We stayed here for about 24 hours and boarded another train for the next destination, Rocky Mount. This same procedure was followed for the next four days until we reached Wilmington and this is where we stayed for the three nights. It was at this location where hundreds of other soldiers were joined with us, it seemed we now numbered close to 500 men.

Finally, we were boarded onto an open flatcar and transferred to the ownership of some Georgia troops. Our destination was now Charleston, where it all began in what seems now to be more than a lifetime ago. At least we could enjoy the fresh air and survey the scenery as we passed along. I began to remember my wanting to take a great adventure when I left Randolph; I was not planning to see this part of the world though. As we entered the city, handsome live oak trees lifted their heads with gray moss surrounding their branches as if they had long beards needing trimming. It was a Sunday and great throngs of people were on the street corners staring at us as we passed by, looking at us as if we were the new pilgrims among them. There were not the taunts and insults we expected. One aged lady, waiting for an opportunity when the guards were not looking came up and gave us something to eat, all the time commiserating our situation. We blessed her for her generosity and enjoyed the small pieces of bread she spared for us. No where else since our capture had any community treated us as well as did Charleston.

We've left this city the next morning and are now heading for Savannah as our next destination. We made good time, but just before the end of our route, we were overtaken by a rain storm, which proved to be quite inconvenient in our unsheltered condition. At Savannah, we changed cars; our destination now was Andersonville, which was to be our home for an indefinite period of time.

This trip was quite long, but at least they only put 35 of us into one car giving us enough room to at least expand for comfort. We traveled about 100 miles and stopped at station No. 13. We were allowed to wash in a brook nearby and to receive very good rations; so good were the rations, we thought we should be fortunate if we could have those in our place of imprisonment. The country in this area was very pleasant, much finer than anything we had yet seen on our trip. We next began our trip to Macon and upon arrival found we were only a short time from our destination.

The Rebel guards gave us favorable descriptions of the location of the prison, speaking of it as being situated in a healthy part of the country, with a fine stream of water running through it, and as to food, they assured us that we would fare well on account of the richness of the State, not being impoverished like many parts of the South. At 9 o'clock at night we arrived at the station outside Andersonville. There is no village and the prison is nearly a mile from the station. We were told to bed down on the ground and rest until morning.

The next morning we were given to new guards from the prison. It is on this night we heard terrible stories of small-pox being prevalent inside the prison, and also about the "dead line," which was death to any one who should step over it, but we concluded they were just trying to frighten us, no place could be that bad.

CHAPTER 9
Andersonville

We were aroused from our slumber early the next morning and called to submit to the orders of a bustling officer, dressed in a captain's uniform, who did his speaking with a great deal of swearing and threats. He divided us into messes of 90 men each; each mess to be in the charge of a sergeant, who should call the roll every morning, draw the rations, and receive an extra one himself for his trouble. Three messes constituted a detachment, which was also in the charge of another sergeant. They took our names within our 90 and we were marched off to the prison. As we drew near, we found the prison to look as though it consisted of about 20 acres of ground, enclosed by a high stockade of hewn pine logs, closely guarded by numerous sentinels, who stood in elevated boxes overlooking the camp.

As we entered the place a spectacle met our eyes that almost froze our blood with horror. Before us were forms that had once been active and erect men, but now they were nothing but mere shape of walking skeletons, covered with filth and vermin. Lemuel exclaimed as he first saw the site, "Can this be hell? God help us." In the center of the whole was a swamp, occupying about three or four acres of the narrowed limits and a part of the swamp looked as though it had been used by the prisoners as a sink. Excrement covered the ground, from which the scent arising was suffocating.

Along the edge of the swamp, from one side of the camp to the other, ran a little sallow brook, three or four feet wide, and this, with a few other small springs, was to furnish our water. There was no shelter provided by our hosts for any prisoners. We therefore went to work to provide our own shelter as best we could. There were 11 of us that had pretty well stuck together from the trip here from Gettysburg. We decided to form a little family. For the small sum of $2 we were allowed to purchase eight small saplings about eight or nine feet long. These we bent and made fast in the ground and we covered them with our blankets, making a tent with an oval roof, about 10 feet square. Blankets were the only thing we had other than our clothes to protect us from the cold at night, but staying out of the rain we thought was more important. In the afternoon we drew rations. Each man received a pint and a half of coarse corn meal, about two ounces of bacon, and a little salt. We built a fire with a little wood given to us and baked a cake for supper using the pans we were given. We then lay down on the hard ground to sleep with no covering. The night was one of the worst I had ever had in my life. The smell of men dying and the excrement wrenched so in my gut, I could sleep very little.

There were ten deaths on our side of the prison the first night we were there. The old prisoners called it "being exchanged," and truly it was a blessed transformation to those who went from such a miserable existence on earth to a glorious one in the sky. Those who died were loaded in a wagon and taken outside the prison where they were buried in a mass shallow grave, having a board placed over their bodies before covering to keep the varmints from digging them up.

Lemuel and I spoke with some of the old prisoners this day, who told us there were about 10,000 of us within the boundaries and we should be particularly aware of the "dead line." All around the inside of the stockade about ten feet from the wall was a slender railing and if one was to trespass over or under this railing accidentally or not would meet with instant death from the vigilant sentinel who was eager for an opportunity to shoot one of us "damned Yankees."

Our small space of perhaps ten feet square of ground was by the brook, near the "dead line." Every morning, before rations were given out, we would have roll call. During roll call men would have to be in ranks and if anyone moved towards the brook or out of line, they were shot.

We have been in the prison for three days and are beginning to find lice on our clothing and it was of no use to attempt to rid ourselves of them for they were everywhere, even crawling on the ground where we slept. To add more fuel to our sorrow and indignation, we were approached by a large gang of men from New York City who were of a mind to rob us of what small possessions we had. Upon their approach to our area, all 11 of us stood up square against them and they turned and retreated back to where they came from.

Lemuel and I resolved ourselves to make rules for our own personal care. We felt that personal cleanliness was to be indispensable for keeping our health in such a place. We decided to visit the brook just before dawn each day before the water had been clouded by others wanting to wash themselves. We swore to each other that if God was willing we were never going to let the rebels have the satisfaction of carrying our bodies out of here in a wagon. Lemuel and I spoke often of our hopes that our friends we left behind in Pennsylvania were not harmed, but if they did not survive, we knew they would be sitting well in the heavens above for they carried with them a good name and substantial honor.

Many a poor, sick man visited this brook to try to bathe themselves well. One poor fellow, who was reduced to a mere skeleton, found himself too weak to drag himself from the water and was obliged to receive help from a comrade. Upon leaving our tent the next morning, I discovered a dead body lying near, and looking more closely saw it to be this same poor fellow who, the evening before, had sought the influence of a bath for his weary frame. He now has met the grim sentry, Death, and has passed over the dark waters to the land of glad immortals.

It is now October and we have heard from newly arriving prisoners that we won the battle of Gettysburg, but a new General was slated to take over the Army, he was General Grant and has a reputation of being a pursuer of the Confederate Army with great zeal. While the news was invigorating it still did not render the facts of our life differently. The one thing we were painfully conscious of, was that a great majority of the residents here were fast going to the silent dead. Every day, 20 or more men, with bodies ravaged from starvation or disease were carried to the prison gates to be loaded on to the death wagon. Strange as it may seem, these ever recurring death scenes had no humanizing effect upon some of our own Union men. It was as if they had become accustomed to such scenes and the gangs of thieves were at the bodies to rob them of whatever mere possessions they may have had before going to their shallow bed of rest.

The confederate guards were passing stories to our men about the possibility of an exchange being negotiated raising all our hopes of being in a better place shortly, then, a few days later they would dispel the rumor and tell us the northern Generals failed in their negotiations. For some reason deception seemed the peculiar delight of our enemy. They seemed to carry an insatiable thirst for revenge inside themselves, perhaps it was to keep us more reconciled, more willing and patient to abide our time, and they did have a constant fear of us, as our numbers were well overwhelming to their numbers watching over us.

Thunderstorms were a frequent visitor to our encampment. Much to our gratification we found that our little tent made of woolen blankets did shed the rain well, but what they would become by the continued beating of the hot sun was a question that deeply concerned us. We 11 were always protective of each other, only traveling in pairs within the prison and always leaving a few of us as guards around our small piece of earth where we lay our heads every night.

The end of October arrived and Lemuel and I formed an acquaintance with a sergeant major from Wisconsin. After a number of weeks and having established a satisfactory relationship, he informed us of a secret organization that is in progress of attempting an outbreak and escape on a grand scale. We told him he might count on us for any such project as it was our wish that we might as well lose our lives in such an attempt as to die by inches in the foul atmosphere of the prison. The plan was to establish a number of tunneling projects at various points around the prison, in this way, traitors inside our own Army who would give up our tunneling efforts to the enemy for an extra ration of food would keep the guards busy actively searching for such tunnels. When the signal would be given, a body of men would rush the stockade in sufficient size as to overturn it, and another body would seize the artillery and turn it upon the rebel camps.

A great deal of planning was involved in this endeavor; it required extreme caution, time and patience and above all, complete unity among those chosen to enter the inner circle of knowledge, for the rebels were eagle-eyed and awake to watching for all possibilities of escape that could be found. Under the pretense of digging for water we would sink a well in some chosen spot and after getting down several feet, abandon it and commence in another place, there were so many wells being dug, the rebels could not know which holes were water wells and which were tunnels.

Of course the work on the tunnel must be done at night and with just such instruments as could be obtained such as knives, spoons, broken canteens—in short anything that could scoop out a handful of earth. To dispose of the earth as fast as it would be taken out, we obtained an old sack, and this was to be filled and passed along to men who were to be stationed at intervals between the point of the tunnel work and another empty hole previously abandoned and could be conveniently filled up. The work was slow and involved many men working a few hours at a time.

It is now November and we have been working the project for over 30 days. A new set of prisoners arrived from the same route as the one we took. There were but a few and immediately upon being left alone as the gates were closed were attacked and robbed by the same band of marauders who still infested the camp and almost completely ruled it. One poor fellow came to an untimely death at their hands and another received a most unmerciful beating because he showed resistance to their inhuman attempts. On the same day a shot rang out from one of the sentries. Upon our investigation, it was discovered that a cripple, who had been living near our tent had crossed the "dead line" and refused to go back, saying he wished to die. The guard fulfilled his wish very quickly, and indeed, if anyone had a desire to shuffle off to the immortal land has only to step inside that line and the work will be done quickly.

Captain Wirz, the commander of the prison was around soon after the shooting with a guard, spying out the land, but we heard nothing of his being enlightened as to our undertaking of the escape plan. I became better acquainted with the ringleaders of the plot. They were a bold set of fellows; most of them had been prisoners for a long time, and had tried to escape several times before. For some reason the rebels were becoming particularly watchful over us, evidently fearing something would escape their notice and they would in some way lose their hold upon us. Very strict orders in regards to escape attempts were read in the camp at morning roll-call. Once again, Captain Wirz told us that negotiations for an exchange were in the works; we chose to not believe him.

There was a great deal of talk among the prisoners about breaking out, but comparatively few knew of the operations in progress to secure such a result. It is now close to the time upon which we are going to hold a great demonstration of the strength and will of the North. The hour of attack was now fixed and as the sun approached the eve of darkness, the stockade was duly cared for, being undermanned at five or six different places. The men were all ready for a general rush upon the artillery and we could only imagine the dismay of the rebels as we relished in our own triumph. The night was auspicious, being dark and rainy, and we ardently hoped everything would favor our scheme. Then, just before the hour for action had arrived we found the whole plot had been disclosed.

One of the ring-leaders had given the entire affair to Captain Wirz. He was supposed to be one of the leaders who was true to his convictions and whom we thought was bound to be faithful to the organization. He was at once taken out of the prison and probably richly rewarded for his information, and it was well this was done for him, for his long continuance on earth might have been a matter of doubt if he had remained among us. Immediately, a large reinforcement of rebel troops arrived to make the guard doubly sure. The stockade was strengthened to resist any type of onslaught by a force of men in the future. We were left despondent and once again, our hopes of leaving this hell hole were left in the wings of a shadow rider as he passes through this unrecoverable period of time.

The next day Captain Wirz ordered a trench to be dug inside the dead line to be of such depth as to discover any tunnels that may be under construction and of course it would be dug by us prisoners. Extra food rations were given to those who would participate and there was no shortage of volunteers. To further punish the prisoners of the entire camp for planning such an escape, the food rations were reduced to two buckets of mush for 90 men per day. It was nothing more than "chicken feed," for it was made up of nothing but coarse corn meal with water and a little salt, half cooked. Even these meager rations were difficult to make their fair share to the masses of men they were to sustain.

Once every day, a large, uncovered Army wagon, drawn by two mules came in through the prison gate. The driver seated upon the near mule and an officer in the vehicle whose business it was to check what was issued to the sergeant who stood ready to take it from another sergeant who stood between them whose responsibility it was to pass the rations out to the 90 men of his division. The 90 had subdivisions so the work of dividing and circulating the rations was done quickly so there was little time for uprisings from the prisoners due to such a small amount of ration being delivered.

It was not unusual for this system to be filled with inequities towards those of us in the masses. Sergeants and thieves would often pocket extra rations for themselves leaving some poor weak fellow on his last legs left with nothing to eat and moving closer to death's door. It would be hard for people outside these grounds to understand what it means to have nothing but a half a loaf of corn bread, weighing about six or seven ounces as the only thing upon which to subsist for 24 hours. This new reduction in rations for the prisoners was done by the order of none other than Captain Werz himself as a penalty to all for the number of tunnels he discovered through his trench program. His actions only increased the hatred we would all draw about us—not only of him as a human being, but also to those who wore the uniform of the South who would allow such a person to be so indignant of others in the human race.

The days continued to move forward and our spirits continued to dwindle. The month of December was filled with a number of days with rain being the order of the day. There were days it would commence in the early part of the day and continue, perhaps slacking just enough to enable us to cook a little. To those who dwell in the tent camps it may not seem a particularly important item, but to those who had no shelter, no alternative but to feel the pitiless torrents upon their stiffened, aching limbs with no bed at night but the cold wet ground, it was a matter of painful disparity. It was oh-so-difficult to watch those thousands trying to shield themselves in every possible way from the fast falling rain and then see them turn hopelessly away and lie down, with their scanty garments already drenched onto Mother Earth's bed. Those who survived would awake to the weariness and pain that can not be removed. Sickness now began to increase immensely throughout the camp and I myself began to feel the consequences of the wet weather. The death count increased so much that three death wagons were brought in every day to haul those out who died from exposure.

In early January the men in our small tent were awarded the opportunity to go outside the and look for wood for the camp. Just the opportunity of breathing pure air was the motivation for me to do this extra work. Lemuel and I worked together once we arrived at our designated location. It almost seemed like we were in another world; my spirit reveled in the glad change of sights for the brief time it was afforded to me. How much better it would have been for us to make our bed under the spreading branches of these pine trees, than to go back to trying to be screened from the chilling dews and falling rain. We carried wood back to the wagons sent out with us and thoroughly enjoyed the day outside the confines of the prison.

Our blankets were now becoming worn and threadbare and afforded us but poor protection from the large rain drops and now we had joined the others in getting a through drenching during those hard rainstorms. No matter how hard this life has made us, Lemuel and I would continue to brighten our day by talking over old home scenes and the jolly times we had with our regiment. We spoke often of our future once we leave this wretched place. We kept our minds in the positive for the fear of not doing so could easily lead one of us to insanity with thoughts of suicide and the satisfaction of our hosts. One man recently stepped over the dead line and was immediately fired upon, but no injury was sustained by him. Instead, two men who were lying down in their tent well inside the line were killed. The man quickly jumped back over the line and melted into the crowd.

Lemuel and I were now getting regular opportunities to go out with the squad to obtain wood. One day we had obtained our scanty supply, and were on our way back to prison when we stopped for a few moments to relieve ourselves. I improved the opportunity to dig all the red root that I could, as it was a valuable remedy for diarrhea, which was distressingly prevalent in camp. The sergeant in charge of the guard was rather cross and surly, and allowed us but a little time to finish and then ordered us on again. In my haste I left my knife upon the ground, and did not discover my loss until I was nearly back to the stockade. The sergeant then refused to let me return for it. I was just about ready to give it up for lost, when Captain Wirz came riding along, and as a last resort I appealed to him. For a wonder he told me to go with him, and, walking his horse, he went with me to the spot where I had used the knife, and thus I recovered it. If I had failed to find it, he would have doubtless thought I was guilty of deception, and shot me through without any remorse whatsoever.

In February, a new set of prisoners arrived and as in the past the camp robbers found fresh opportunities to continue their devious work. They seized one of the new arrivals and after severely beating and cutting his head; they took from him his watch and $175 in paper. His demeanor was one who did not bother with his own security from this gang and he entered a complaint with Captain Wirz who caused the whole camp to be aroused. He authorized a crowd of men to obtain clubs and begin to arrest the entire gang as fast as possible. As soon as one was caught, he was handed outside to the care of the Rebels, who were to watch over them until they could be tried by our men. A few, against whom positive proof could not at once be brought, were sent back into the prison where they had to run the gauntlet between a long line of enraged men, who, armed with heavy clubs, dealt blows at them as they ran past. One man was killed while undergoing this punishment.

A gallows had been erected on the south side of the prison, and it was said that half a dozen of the men arrested as camp robbers, who had been tried and found guilty, were to be hung. At 4:30 in the afternoon, Captain Werz came in with the six scoundrels under a rebel guard, and turned them over to the Vigilance Committee. They were convicted of murder and robbery and were sentenced to be hung until they were dead.

Upon giving them up for punishment, the captain made the following remarks: "These men have been tried and convicted by their own fellows, and I now return them to you in as good condition as I received them. You can do with them as your reason, justice, and mercy dictates. And may God protect both you and them."

The Catholic priest begged hard that their lives might be spared, but finding himself unsuccessful in this, he turned his attention to their spiritual condition, and spent a session in prayer for them. The men themselves seemed strangely unconcerned, apparently thinking it was simply an affair to thoroughly frighten them, and they appeared to cling to the idea, even as they had ascended the platform erected for their execution. As they were about to mount the scaffold, one of them broke from the men who were holding him, and ran through the crowd, across the swamp, to the opposite hill-side, as if by one desperate effort he would escape his fearful doom. However, he was captured, led back and he was securely placed with the other five.

Opportunity was given them to speak, if they had anything they wished to say before their final minutes expired. None of them said much and then meal sacks were placed over their heads, the fatal ropes were adjusted and as they were pushed off the scaffold the rope around the neck of the leader of the gang broke, thus setting him free. He was at once taken back up, had the rope readjusted and was pushed off. The entire six were sent to their eternal world. Their depredations had been carried on so long and with such a bold hand that it was necessary for an example be made of them in this way, leaving a lasting impression upon all those who should be similarly inclined.

It is now the middle of winter and even though we are in the deep south, our tent begins to lose some of its members. One cool January day at about 5:00 in the afternoon, a beloved comrade who had traveled so far and for so long with us spoke to us no more. I can never again forget the vacant expression on the face of my dead brother as his glazed eyes seemed to focus on a sight we have yet to see.

It is now the end of February and again we are inundated with news that an exchange was in the works; however, our energy for excitement has become weak and our enthusiasm for reaching out to hope for our disparity has been just about dissolved.

The month of March was a welcome sight to those of us who could continue to move around. We now have no shoes and must sloth about in our bare feet, but when we are called upon for wood duty, none of us are too weak to leave the fortress and venture into Mother Nature's den. One day when we were out on wood detail I had a conversation with one of our guards.

He told me with great frankness, "I reckon you 'uns fare pretty hard inside, but we ain't to blame for it. The ol' captain is as hard on us as he is with you. A heap of us was taken right off our farms, and we left the crops standing, with nobody to tend 'em but the women folks. This was the way the southern men was conscripted. No wonder ol' Jeff Davis keeps his Army full; it's die fighting or die refusing to fight."

Many of the guards thought we had invaded the South simply to take their farms from them. That has been what was preached to them for a number of years by the big politically-motivated plantation owners.

I have managed to buy a pair of shoes from one of the newly arrived prisoners, for my own comfort, but it was the first time I had worn any for three months. Lemuel still had no shoes, but he refused to spend his hard saved money for shoes; he would rather hold on out of fear of a need to buy a meager amount of food if we were cut off completely. Being in the spring season, we were often visited by thunderstorms and it was not unknown for the lightning to strike the tall pine trees in close proximity to us. We now had nothing to shield us from the rain, for our blanket tents had come to be of little worth, except to shelter us from the afternoon sun.

Of our original band of 11, we now have only 8 and as I take reflection of those of us who are still breathing, I could notice the change in our behavior and personalities that has taken place in all of us. When we first entered, we thought our stay would be of a short nature and an exchange would be taking place and we tried to pass the time away as pleasantly as possible. We used to sit in the clear evenings and sing patriotic songs, but now everybody looked without care and moved about quietly and sadly.

One young man of excellent education, while in this sad condition would go down to the little brook nearly every day at noon, when the heat of the sun was most intense, he would take off all his rags and wade back and forth, but never washed himself. Finally, after seeing this over and over again, Lemuel and I walked down to him.

"Why don't you wash yourself and come out and not stay in the hot sun so long?" I asked.

His hopeless reply was, "I am waiting for the water to become clear."

Poor fellow, the water of this brook would never become clear, so he continued to just walk back and forth.

As we were visiting our poor brother, another man was wallowing in the stench of the swamp. He seemed to imagine he was some sort of animal and he would strip himself of all clothing and persist in beating the swamp on his hands and knees.

These were things that were happening to us, but as we walked back to our little campsite, we saw something that no man should bear witness to. Another poor fellow was lying on the ground under his propped up blanket which was held up by four sticks about a foot long. He was alive, but he was being devoured by maggots. Parts of his body were eaten until they had become raw and bloody, and they could even be seen issuing from his mouth as he lay there with barely a shallow breath being taken. We found out that this poor fellow was with Company A of the 52nd New York Infantry and he came to this terrible state through sickness, exposure and neglect. I thought to myself, if I should live to get North again, I would never speak of these horrors, for they would seem too much for any person to believe, even though these are the realities we live under day after day.

With the winter slowly receding, rumors were floating about that an exchange was in process. These rumors have been persistent before as supplied by our unfriendly guards, but this time it was reported to us at the morning call by Captain Wirz. This began to give us a new sign of hope and that little bit of hope raised our minds from the thoughtless process of dying a slow death. But this deliverance for us could not come too fast, as two more of our tent comrades died last night. One fellow was only 15 years of age, who never ought to have been admitted into the service. He was a brave boy, and felt quite proud that he was enduring his imprisonment as well as he did for a time, but the sickness of sleeping on the cold ground during a rainstorm had consumed his body and he woke no more from his sleep. As with this young man, another fellow, a corporal with the Connecticut regiment, succumbed to death's visit during the same night. He closed his eyes upon the earthly scenes just as the rest of us did at twilight. Now his name has been stricken from the roll-call of prison and added to the long list of sleeping heroes treasured outside these gates.

It was known that I became quite concerned over my friend Lemuel. He has taken sick from the constant living under Mother Nature's umbrella and has the shakes. He refuses to take sick call when the roll is read in the mornings, for the fear inside him of going to the hospital outside the camp was that no one seemed to ever come back; it was considered a death march to go there. Yet, I could not let my friend deteriorate into another casualty of this godforsaken place. Finally, I convinced him to go to the hospital and I would also say I am sick and go with him. That way, I could at least be with him and hopefully he could get some relief from the ailment eating away at his innards. We both knew the odds of him coming out of the hospital alive were against him, but in this filthy place it was sure death to stay where he was. So we lined up and marched to the hospital.

Upon heading towards the hospital I noticed from a distance that no walls were around the tents erected; only pieces of canvas on a center pole sheltered those poor sick and dying men. When entering the tents, the soldiers here were of the worst I have ever seen, their emaciated, pain-racked frames had no place to rest but upon the cold, hard ground, and in most instances their heads were pillowed upon nothing softer than a stick of wood. The skin would often wear away, leaving their bodies sore, and these men could not be cared for, as there was nothing to dress them with.

Add to this the impurity of the air they breathed. A hole in the ground had been dug in the middle of the tent with a drain to the outside of the field beside the tent, this is where all the excrement of mankind would go. The air alone was enough to make any healthy human being sick.

We were now the property of the physicians. Many of these people had no feeling whatsoever for the prisoners as they were conscripts themselves. They chose this profession rather than shoulder a musket and go to the front. They were given 11 Confederate dollars a month and a daily ration of meat and bacon. They availed themselves of the opportunity to acquaint themselves with surgery, and were not therefore slow in performing amputations if they saw fit. They also had a dissecting house not very far away, where they continued their experiments.

The physicians commenced their duties at about 8:00 in the morning and finished about 1:00 in the afternoon. Overall, they were kind to us in a general sense of the word. However, they would not enter the tents to speak or touch the patients. They would stand at the opening and ask us how we felt and give the clerk a prescription to give to us. The doctor of our ward was a Georgian—a fine fellow; he was one of the rare people with whom I felt a comfort with. He was not vindictive by nature and truly tried his best to help the sick men in our ward. He was especially kind to Lemuel, who began to rally somewhat after receiving a few days of prescriptions along with some white oak, sweet fern, and sumac berries, which relieved his diarrhea.

But even by finding one decent person in this hell hole did not relieve us of the knowledge that cruelty and heartlessness was still among us. One night, while resting on the ground in our ward, a young man arose and walked to a fire that was kept by the guards who were stationed around the hospital. The guard yelled gruffly, "Get away from there," and before the young man had a chance to obey and retreat, he fired his musket and ended his days. This was not an isolated case; you took a chance on survival when moving about any time after the sun goes down. Everyday, men would die and more men would arrive. When death did come, the nurses, who were conscripts, would go through the dead man's pockets, keeping all that was materially this man's property before turning the body over to the guards.

The men inside the tents with us suffered from diarrhea, scurvy, dropsy, or typhoid; we were fortunate to have been able to go to the hospital in the early stages of our illness and have a good doctor. We were getting a little strength back and becoming ready to be released back to the prison when we started checking on the conditions of some of the men in our tent.

One man who was suffering from diarrhea had not eaten anything for a week except a little flour paste, while all the time his evacuations would be nothing but blood and with the most excruciating pain until he passed out.

A second man who had dropsy, had limbs so swollen they would burst, and for the desire of proper treatment would be filled with insects. The man next to him and also with the same disease would cry out constantly from the pain for someone to kill him. Scurvy was of a horrible state to witness, many men carried the disease. Some could not walk as their limbs would be drawn up tight. Others would have the disease on their insides and would produce tremendous pain and other times it would be in the mouth, and the gums would become separated from the teeth, and finally the teeth would drop out altogether causing a man to starve to death because he could no longer eat the course food given him.

The blood of these men was in such an impure state, that the least break of the skin would be almost sure to lead to a gangrenous sore, and many amputations were performed. Under the influence of a scorching sun, the entire upper surface of the skin would become blistered, then break open, leaving the flesh exposed, and having nothing to dress it with, or protect it in any way, gangrene was inevitable. A few days went by and Lemuel and I were released to go back into the prison. I said farewell to the doctor and praised him for healing us and especially my friend, Lemuel, for without him I doubt we would have the strength to continue on in this place.

Upon returning to the prison, we heard that a few of the men had been told by Captain Wirz of their upcoming pardon and to be prepared to leave the camp for an exchange. What excitement rushed through our bodies! We had so many questions, but the most important one on our minds was how were the men chosen? The answer seemed to be: by the Captain himself. Now it became an issue of how this Captain could ever ascertain our names from the thousands of men here. Another discouragement hung over our heads as we laid ourselves down to once again sleep on this terrible earth.

The next morning at roll call, we were told that five thousand men would be leaving over the next several days and what was left of our 90 would be one of them,.As a matter of chance, we would be leaving the very next day. Lemuel and I just hugged each other and those around us who were able to stand and cheer as loudly as possible. All our dreams and prayers for well over six months had been answered and all I could see in my mind was Emma's face—a face whose beauty I thought many times I would never see again.

The next morning we were divided into squads of 60 men each and marched over to the depot. The sick ones were placed between the strongest of us, who bore them up, and in this manner we worked our way slowly along the road. As we were passing the headquarters of Captain Werz, he cried out to us, "You'll never come back here again!" and while afraid to blurt it out, we all felt like saying, "I hope we never do." Upon our arrival at the depot, we were immediately loaded into the boxcars, a squad of 60 in each, with two guards on top. Inside we found some corn bread and bacon, which we were told was our allowance for two days, and also two wooden buckets in which we were to get our supply of water at the different stopping places.

After about two hours of loading men into boxcars, the locomotive's whistle finally blew its beautiful music and we started off. YES! we were really leaving behind us this plague spot upon the fair earth. There had been no better feeling in our lives than at this moment. We arrived in Macon early the next morning. There were some men among us who did not believe there was to be an exchange and thought we were just being moved to another prison. They made their escape while in Macon and the guards on the roof of the boxcars fired their muskets. We don't know if they were hit or not as the train had already started on its way to Savannah.

From Savannah, we switched tracks and continued to move towards Charleston. Upon arrival in Charleston, we were marched to the shore docks where a number of vessels had been moored. As we sat in a large holding area waiting to board one of the many steamers being prepared for departure, we noticed out in the distant harbor a large steamer, which had apparently dropped anchor. It had an American Flag flying from the rigging and even through it was a large distance away, it was impossible for us to gaze upon that precious emblem of Freedom with dry eyes. It was a touching sight to see the upturned faces, the eager gaze of our men. Never before was that flag so dear to our hearts. How insignificant and contemptible in comparison was the flaunting Rebel rag that had so long been displayed to us.

We were finally loaded upon one of the vessels, the Star of the South, and departed the dock at Charleston. We then steamed closer to the large ship with our American flag so proudly being displayed and it wasn't long before we were alongside her. Lemuel and I just looked at each other without having to speak any words, for both of us were feeling the same emotion of relief as they lay down the plank connection by which we would transfer. As we boarded the large steamer, I asked the sailor the name of this vessel, he replied, "Why, it's the New York of course." I never knew I could hear any brighter words than those spoken by this man.

Shortly after boarding we were called upon to divest ourselves of our wretched garments and throw them all away, and we saw the miserable rags float down the river without the least feeling of regret, and with them, our old companions, the lice. We washed ourselves in water dipped from the cold river, and though it caused some shivering, we were heartily glad of the opportunity to be clean once more. As fast as this was done, we were marched in a row to the counter, where each man was given a new suit of Uncle Sam's blue and a good pair of shoes. Then, we were marched off to the galley, where we received our first meal of Army food, and what a feast it was. We could not find words strong enough to express our admiration and with a full pint of coffee to boot. I doubted if there was ever a happier crowd than we that night. Some danced, others sang and everyone was full of jokes and good humor.

The next morning, we weighed anchor and left the Confederacy for the more pleasant scenes of our northern homes, getting back to God's country. But our pleasant atmosphere and feeling of contentment was short lived, because as we passed Fort Pulaski and headed out upon the ocean, there came up a fresh gale of wind and the sea became rough. Lemuel and I both headed for the side of the ship giving departure to all the good things that had so warmly been consumed a short time before. The regular sailors enjoyed the rough conditions and seemed to look upon us with contempt because of our inability to endure so little a discomfort. After a number of hours the seas quieted down again and for the next two days we sailed in pleasant seas for our port at Annapolis. As we were arriving at the dock we were greeted with "Hail Columbia" from the Marine Band and its cheering strains never fell upon the ears of a more grateful group of listeners. We were soon on shore and well cared for; we received two months pay and commutations of rations for the time we had been in prison at the rate of 25 cents per day, followed by a full 30-day furlough. The spring days of March allowed Lemuel and I ample opportunity to visit home and recoup with our family and friends. My mind began to focus on nothing more than seeing Emma once again. My God, I have thought many times over the last six months how I may never see her face again except through the waiting arms at the gates of St. Peter.

Before leaving for home, we were able to get an update on where the Army was and the current condition of the War. We were told at the present time the command of the Army was changed to General Grant as rumor had reported to us while in prison. One of General Grant's first orders was to cease all exchanges of prisoners. He believed the North had a superior population to draw replacements from and the South was limited. Thus, further exchanges would enhance the southern Army to continue to fight this war longer. Our exchange was to be the last exchange of prisoners for the remaining days of the war. God help those poor men who were left behind.

As Lemuel and I left the train station in Annapolis heading for Randolph, we were able to see the strains of this prolonged war on the faces of all the people we would come into contact with along the way. While we were happy to be going home to see our folks, we longed for the opportunity to return to our brothers who still remained at the front. While our suffering was long and hard, we both felt uneasy to be taking leave from the war because we had been disposed of for the past six months. But our desire to visit our family and friends was so great that we both took advantage of the leave offered. I could only think of seeing my beloved Emma as quickly as possible.

CHAPTER 10
The Final Six Months

As we arrived at the station in Randolph, the village seemed to be almost deserted. It was early in the morning when the train pulled into the station and a steady spring rain was falling. We didn't have time to properly mail our intentions to anyone as the mail would have been slower than our physical arrival. Mr. Crowley was putting goods outside his store as Lemuel and I walked over to him. As we walked towards him, he looked up.

"Oh my God! Thank God both you boys are still alive, we had almost given up hope of you getting back, and you both look plum terrible."

"Well, we sure haven't been eating properly for the past six months, but we've perked up some in the last couple of weeks. We are in need of something a little more valuable to us than food right now," Lemuel said.

"What is it you boys need?"

"We need to find some means of getting Lemuel home to his wife and child and I need to get out to the Sholtz farm," I replied.

Mr. Crowley looked at us and laughed. "Go out back boys where my rig is tied up and I will have William take both of you to your destinations."

We gave him our gratitude for his kindness and within a few moments we were off.

I had made up my mind on the train trip home that my first stop would be to my beloved Emma. It wasn't that I didn't want to see my folks or siblings, but Emma had been on my mind constantly since we entered Andersonville and she was the main reason I was able to withstand the hardships of that hell hole. Lemuel lived out further from town than Emma's folks, so I was the first to be dropped off. I said my farewells to Lemuel and told him I would meet him at the station on April 23rd for our return trip to the regiment. I then thanked William and started to walk down the farm lane towards Emma's folk's house.

As I walked up the lane, I began to feel queasiness in my stomach; I began to think about how long it had been without having any communication. I began to have doubts in my mind that perhaps I was forgotten or that someone else had stepped in to the center of her attention. Perhaps a wounded soldier she had helped to recover from his wounds swept her off her feet? I began to sweat profusely wondering what to expect when our eyes did finally meet. I stepped up on the porch and knocked on the door and did not receive an answer. I then began to think that perhaps she was out again on one of her missions to help the wounded soldiers returning home. I knocked again, and this time I heard footsteps approaching the door. It opened and there she stood, as beautiful as I had remembered. As she saw me a gleam lit her face and she threw herself upon me wrapping her arms completely around my now small-framed body.

"Careful," I said laughingly, "I'm as dusty and sweaty as a mule."

"Sweaty, dusty, I don't care what condition you are in as long as you are alive," and with that she placed a long, sweet kiss on my dry mouth. It was as refreshing as water from a mountain well. She locked her hands behind my neck while we embraced and I felt the lushness of her full figure against me. Her response took away any misgivings I may have had about her giving me up for dead.

I remained at her folks' farm for the next two days. Emma's parents were very accommodating, allowing me a stall in the barn during the night, which was fine with both Emma and I as we had our privacy away from the house and the rest of her family. I ate substantially while there and after two days of rest and good food, I bid myself farewell for a small period of time and Emma took me over to my parents' farm.

Ma had already heard of my arrival in Randolph and while she was not happy that I didn't come home right away, she was very pleased to see me anyway. As I arrived with Emma, she came out of the house.

"Boy, have you no respect for your poor Mother, leaving her to worry about you so?" she scolded, and at the same time gave me a big hug and a kiss on my forehead.

"Ma, it's not that I didn't miss seeing you and Pa, it's just I had to see Emma first."

"Well, since it was Emma and not some other woman, I guess I can forgive you. Your Pa is back behind the barn mending a fence—you better go say hello to him."

I turned and began walking towards the back of the barn while Emma and Ma went inside to the kitchen. Pa was nailing some rails into a fence post as I turned the corner behind the barn and he never saw me approach. I quietly came up to him.

"Would you like another pair of hands to help you with this?" I asked.

He turned, looked at my face, eyed me up and down, and then replied, "You don't look much like you're able to help anyone do anything. What the hell happened to you boy?" Then he took my hand and shook it heartily, which is about as close as I've ever seen Pa to having any emotion over a person. He just wasn't that way, but I could tell he was happy to see me.

"Pa, I think I have been to Hell and back and I'm damn glad to have left that place, for the Devil is not where the Good Book says; he's right down in the state of Georgia."

Pa looked at me and said, "Son, do you want to tell me about it?"

"Not right now Pa. Maybe someday soon I can talk about it, but right now, I would like to just get my health back and enjoy a little home life before I have to go back to my regiment."

"That's ok, boy. Let's take a break and go up to the house and see what Ma has on the stove."

So, we left, both walking side by side, not saying a word, but I knew Pa would give me the respect of my silence; he was just that kind of man.

Emma and I spent the rest of the day with my parents and after supper, I broke the news to them that we planned on getting married when my enlistment was up come next September. They seemed very pleased with my choice and wished us both well. We then loaded ourselves back into the buggy and headed back to Emma's home to tell her parents of our news to marry. Along the way Emma and I spoke of the war and what it has done to people in the community and the losses of such good friends we both knew.

"James, you know I must continue my work treating the returning soldiers until they are back on their feet, even after we are married."

Of course I knew she would have to continue this practice; her heart and soul was always with others as she doesn't have a selfish bone in her body.

I simply replied, "Emma, as long as there is room in your heart for me every once in a while, I guess I can tolerate sharing you until this war is finally put to rest. But after that, I would think we'd be looking to start a family and take care of ourselves."

She didn't reply right away, just sort of sat there staring ahead. I knew she had begun to think again about the wounded men at the convalescent home who had returned home maimed and near death's door. We spoke no more about this subject while I was home and I was glad of it.

The rest of the 30-day leave was spent between Emma's home when she was there and recovering my health through the natural elements of Ma's good cooking. It was getting close to April 23rd and I knew I had to meet Lemuel at the station to begin our trip back to the front with our regiment. While I missed seeing my friends in the ol' 64th, I had a stronger desire to stay forever with my Emma, but I could never reveal this feeling as it would be considered treason amongst the community to not return to those who are still sacrificing their souls for the good of the country.

As Emma and I approached the station in Randolph, the skies had just started to darken and a spring storm was definitely imminent. I jumped off the buggy and said, "You should return home as quickly as possible as I suspect this rain will be coming in a matter of hours."

She just looked at me and then climbed down off the buggy, came over and embraced me and said, "You must be careful wherever you may go; here is something to remember me by." And with that she handed me a sprig of dried mountain laurel that had been pressed in a book. I inserted the laurel in my breast pocket and kissed my dear Emma good bye.

When I turned to leave, I said to her, "It is not me the Rebs want to deal with anymore; it is their own shameless souls that has them befuddled." Then I turned and headed towards the station steps.

When Lemuel and I met at the station, I could see the sadness in his face.

"This is the hardest thing I think I have ever had to do in my life."

I didn't know what to say. He was married with a small child who had grown in the past two years without knowing her Pa. Finally, after a few moments, I turned to him.

"Look Lemuel, this war has to end soon and we only have about six more months before our enlistment is up. We both don't want to go back, but we must. We could never live with the shame of not completing our duty."

He looked at me and said, "I know; it's just that I may have seen the last of my family, for I ain't gonna get captured no more. I've had enough of that; if it gets close, they will have to kill me first." His look was serious and I knew he meant what he said.

"Let's not think about being captured; let's just get through to September and get back home."

The ride back to Washington was monotonous now; and even though it was on the same train line as the original trip some years ago, it wasn't the same. My mind now only contained visions of my beloved Emma and returning home to her instead of the visions I had in the past when traveling this trip—of getting into a fight with the Rebs and leading the charge to a tremendous victory. Victory in my mind was now far away—if it ever could be realized. I've seen the pain of men dying more than I want to remember; I've seen the results of what poor leadership can bring to an Army. I've seen in my friend's eyes the suffering of being away from his family for such a long period of time and I've have felt the pain of leaving something so special behind to once again march off to the possibility of one's death, never to speak again directly to those you love so much. It was quiet without much to talk about as we listened to the constant clicking of the wheels of the train going clickety-clack, clickety-clack as we continued our journey on this adventure I now regret ever taking.

As we arrived in Washington, we learned that our regiment was camped at Stevensburg, Virginia, preparing for the spring campaign. We hurriedly made preparations for transportation to our camp and within two days had arrived at our destination. As we approached the camp we noticed it had changed from the camps we had been accustomed to. The tents were small, just fitting enough for two men to lie down inside and the soldiers seemed to be younger and green and didn't have the enthusiasm of the soldiers of the past. After searching for some time we found our long lost friends who welcomed us with open arms. Frank Jones was the first to come up to me and place his hand outright to grab mine.

"Thank the good Lord, James, you made it through," he said smiling. He was now a first sergeant as was Albert Marsh, who also came up to us right away.

"Boy," I said, "you boys sure did move up in the ranks since we've been gone."

"Oh, it's not us moving up as much as there not being many men here with experience to try to keep these young drafters alive during a fight," replied Albert.

Then there was Franklin Higbe, the one-arm cook who was more dedicated then ever to continuing his service for his country. He came over and we shook left hands while he glared at us.

"You boys hungry? I got a few victuals on the spit over here," he said.

"After where I've been the last six months, I am always in a hungry mood," I replied.

We then sat down by the camp fire and listened to the stories about the condition of the Army and the change in leadership again. Before Frank got started with his tales, I asked him, "How many of the original 43 are with us today?"

He looked at me for a while as if he were counting the bodies in his head and said, "I think 13 of us are left, and that includes you and Lemuel. I don't know how many there will be after this next move we are about to undertake. My God, I hope this thing ends soon."

Frank and Albert went on to explain to us that General Meade did not pursue the Rebel Army after Gettysburg, and Lincoln was furious. A General named Grant had taken many victories in the west and Lincoln had now made him Lt. General of all the Armies. He has been known to be a man who does not quit fighting until he has slain the enemy in full.

General Grant has laid out new plans on how to end this war," Frank continued. "He has sent General Sherman's Army south from western Virginia towards Savannah with instructions to burn every town, farm, railroad, and bridge, and to take all livestock in his path. His goal is to cut off all their supply routes and not stop until he reaches the sea. He also told the Secretary of War that there will be no more prisoner exchanges. The General believes the north has a larger population base with which to replace soldiers and all the exchanges were doing is prolonging the war by having released rebels return to the fight."The final plan lies with us—the Army of the Potomac. We will no longer focus on the capturing of Richmond. We will now focus on destroying Lee's Army wherever he may go. We will encircle him with our larger Army and constrict him into submission. He will either have to fight his way out or starve to death. General Butler is marching his Army up the James River from the east, General Sigel is moving up the Shenandoah Valley to cut off their supplies from the west and we are to attack Lee head-on from the north."

After listening for a while to what Frank was saying, I asked him, "What are we to do?"

"We've been preparing for a movement to surround Lee once Sherman is well on his way to destroying the southern supply lines and word has it we are about to begin that movement within a few days."

We spoke for a few hours more and then I decided it was time to send a letter to Emma and the folks to let them know I had arrived safely. As I began to write to Emma, I began to feel a sense of my insides being pulled in two different directions. My heart ached to be away from Emma, but my duty and commitment was with my friends in settling this war once and for all. I wrote to Emma about the possibility of going into action in a few days and I told her I would always be carrying the dried sprig of mountain laurel in my coat pocket for good luck. I did promise her I would not re-enlist when my time ran out come next September and would be home for a big fall wedding. I closed my letters and looked around the camp; it was getting dark now and the older veterans were beginning to settle into the tents while the younger drafters were still playing cards, drinking, and carrying on just like we'd done some years before. I reflected back to those days when we first left Cattaraugus County and couldn't wait to get into the fight. Now, I pray for the fighting to end and to return to some sense of life without war. As I lay down to fall into some resting sleep, the last thing I remembered was the icy tone of the Captain Wirz of the prison shouting out, "You boys don't want to come back here!"

A few days later Lemuel and I were back into the regular routines of Army life, taking our turns on picket duty and drilling with the new recruits, most of whom were Irish and from New York City. Our old Corp had been torn up so much at Gettysburg that it was consolidated with the 3rd Corp into one unit. It wasn't the same; the enthusiasm of the men was slight to say the least and the officers were almost like taskmasters to get the new recruits to respond as a fighting group. It was as if the spirit to win was leaving us; it would have to take a strong leader to finish off Lee, and I really hoped Grant had what it will take.

I could tell Lemuel was not happy with the new recruits who had infiltrated our company. While they were from the state of New York, they were of the worst character. Many of these men were drafted—some directly from prison or immigrants right off the boats arriving in the New York harbor. They carried no enthusiasm for our cause whatsoever. They had no discipline, or respect for our officers and many of them tried to desert. Over the next few days our company was given the task of providing guard duty to those would-be deserters. It was during this time that my friend became involved in an episode of disgrace to his honor.

Each one of us was assigned to guard two deserter prisoners awaiting their turn to have their face cheeks branded with a hot iron with the letter "D" and then made to walk home. My duty was during the daylight hours and Lemuel's was during the night. Early one morning, Lemuel returned to our camp and during breakfast exclaimed that one of his prisoners escaped during the night.

"How did you let that happen?" I asked.

"It wasn't my fault; he had to pee, so I let him lean up against a tree. While I turned away to tend to the other prisoner who was complaining of the lack of water, the first prisoner took off through the woods."

"Lemuel, this is not good. You know this is a different Army now and Grant has issued orders he will not tolerate slackers."

"James, I'm tired of this war; I'm tired of these new recruits who cry like babies because they are here with us; I'm tired of officers leaning on us veterans to carry the whole load and I'm just plain worn out. I don't care what happens to me anymore."

The rest of the day we heard of nothing regarding the escape and Lemuel slept well. Upon my arrival back to camp from my watch I saw two officers speaking with Lemuel. After they departed, I asked him what they wanted.

"Well, I've been relieved from guard duty and returned to picket duty until they sort this whole incident out."

We both agreed that wasn't a bad solution if that is all that came from it. But it wasn't. Three days later, those same two officers returned to our camp with four soldiers. The officers told Lemuel that the escapee was caught hiding at a brothel about ten miles away. They also told him the escapee claimed that Lemuel deliberately let him go and they were there to arrest him and take him before the Provost Judge for trial.

Lemuel turned to the rest of us and said, "Don't worry boys, this will be squared away in a short while," and then they marched off. The rest of us just stared at their backs as they took our friend away, we knew it was not going to be easy for him as the new Army has little tolerance for dereliction of duty. Soldiers falling asleep on picket duty were now being shot by a firing squad. In the early days, each regiment would be allowed to judge and issue their own discipline orders as all the soldiers came from the same vicinity. But now, the consolidation of so many men into different regiments meant the creation a central court for each Corp.

I found out when Lemuel's trial would be and made sure I would not be on any duty that day, and Albert was doing the same. We figured we could at least testify on Lemuel's behalf as to his character and past history—after all, he was promoted to Corporal. These trials were short in nature and there were many of them taking place each day. The General in charge seemed to be unfit to the task of listening and making his decisions based on the testimony given to him as all the men before Lemuel were found guilty in a quick response at the end of all testimony. We feared the worst and our fears became reality. Lemuel told his story to the General, then the escapee who was now branded on his cheek testified and said that Lemuel told him to shut up and quit whining, as he was tired of listening to yellow bellies and cowards and if he didn't shut up he was going to shoot him. Then the escapee said he offered Lemuel $10 to turn his back and let him go. He said Lemuel agreed to it, let him loose to go pee and turned his back so he could escape. The General looked at Lemuel and he just sat there and didn't say anything. The General asked him if he had anything to say to which Lemuel would not respond. He just stared straight ahead and said nothing. The General then made his decision quickly, found Lemuel guilty and sentenced him to 90 days of hard labor with a 24-pound ball attached to his leg so he couldn't escape.

As he left the tent under guard, he turned to us and said his goodbyes.

"Don't worry—doing 90 days will be like a rest compared to what I've already been through. Once these 90 days are over, I will only be 30 days from the end of my enlistment. I will see you again, James, but next time it will be back home."

Then he turned and walked away. I could not believe what had just happened here; it was as if Lemuel had wanted the General to find him guilty. I knew he was distraught about leaving his family and returning to the war as I was, but I had no idea how distraught he had really become. I truly believe now that he was searching for a way to make sure he would return to his wife and child alive and to leave this life of human destruction forever. Now I have lost my tent partner and best friend with still four months remaining on my enlistment. Frank Jones, Albert Marsh, and one-armed Franklin Higbe and I were now all that remained from our group of eight that started out in what seems like an eternity ago.

The next day I received a new tent mate, a short stocky young man about 16 years old from New York City. He told me his name, but he said everyone just calls him "Buckwheat." He was a chatterer, and said the only reason he was here was because he made a shady deal with a draftee who paid him to take his place. He figured he wasn't old enough to be drafted yet and by the time he was the war would be over and he would have missed out on all the excitement—plus this way he could make some money at it as well.

I looked at him and said, "So, you think this is going to be a fun little game, eh? Just wait until you see the elephant, then let me know how much fun you are having."

He turned and said with a smile, "Relax James, Buckwheat is here now, we'll have this thing over and be home in time for dinner."

I just looked at him in bewilderment and shook my head thinking to myself, this babe has a lot to learn; I hope he lives long enough to learn his lesson correctly.

The next day, May 3rd, 1864, we received the order from General Hancock to prepare to break camp and march out at midnight. The word had spread that Longstreet was not with Lee and was protecting the crucial railroad junction at Gordonsville, some 25 miles to the west. The plan called for us to move against Lee before Longstreet's Corp could be recalled, but we had to march through the wilderness to get to the right of Lee's Army. A year earlier almost to the day we were at the same location near Chancellorsville. That time we fought in the thickness of the wilderness without having the aid of artillery and lost terribly. This time the plan would be to do our fighting a few miles west of the wilderness where the artillery can do the most to help the attack.

We began our march toward Elys Ford and continued until we arrived at the crossing about daybreak. The cavalry was well in advance and already across the pontoon bridge before we arrived. As we crossed the bridge we set out for Chancellorsville and arrived there about 9:00 am and halted along the Plank road. It was at this place we established our camp for the night—on the same battleground we had fought on just one year earlier. After we made camp, Albert and I walked over to the remaining breastworks we had fought from in the battle last year.

"Remember those Rebs charging at us from those woods," he said, as he pointed to the group of trees directly south of us.

"Of course I do; how can I forget it? I also remember we were out of bullets and they were still coming. I still don't know why they cut off their charge when they did, but I sure am glad they did."

Albert looked around and then he turned and said, "You know we got a lot of green boys with us, many of whom have never seen the elephant. We've got to be careful what we do. I don't want a bullet from the wrong side to end up in one of our backs. I don't think I have ever seen a worst bunch of recruits as we have now."

I stared a long time at the woods. "I know; I have my concerns as well."

It was 3:00 in the morning and we were up and ready to march. This time we were loaded for a fight. We moved out towards Shady Grove Church and Todd's Tavern and halted at about 9:00 am. A message was received that the enemy was seen advancing towards us on the Wilderness Road. That means Lee had discovered our movement and was preparing to attack us while we were in the wilderness again, hoping to stall our march until Longstreet could arrive. We stopped along the narrow Brock Road where it met the Orange Plank Road. Lee had sent Ewell's Army to attack our right flank and A.P. Hill's Army to attack our left flank. We were no longer in control of the location of the dance; the enemy was bent on taking us on in the thickness of these woods once again. We began quickly to build breastworks; the trees around us were dry or dead from the battle a year ago, so they were easy to bring down, and by 2:00 pm we had ourselves pretty well dug in. General Getty's division of the 6th Ccorp was to our right and we held the left end of our Army's line.

It was around 4 o'clock in the afternoon. Hill had two divisions directly in front of General Getty's division about 300 yards, but was not yet attacking. It was then that General Meade issued the order for General Getty to attack, which he did and while we were not yet immediately engaged, we could hear the sounds of battle as clear as if they were right beside us. The infamous Rebel yell mixed with the continued bombardment of musketry left a field of smoke and fire so thick we could only guess what was actually happening. Within half an hour, we received orders from General Hancock to attack the Rebel line and turn them right. I stood up, looked at Albert and we each nodded. There was no need to say anything; we knew it was certainly possible we would not escape the battle alive—it was as if we were acknowledging to each other a long acquaintance if we should not see one another again.

Our regiment stood up and Colonel Brooke ordered us to move forward and prepare for close fighting. As we moved through the thickness of the brush, we found it difficult to advance with any speed and we were pretty much just following the sounds of war to our right. Then, they appeared through the smoke: men fighting hand to hand, fist to fist. Colonel Brooke then ordered us to charge and we started yelling and trying to run through the woods to join the fight. Many of the young recruits in their first battle fired the muskets into the center of the fighting not knowing who they were aiming at and I am now sure they killed many a man in the blue. The music of the battle was intense; pine trees were on fire bellowing smoke that almost choked both sides of the combatants. Trees were falling from being cut with so many balls of musketry. One ball found its mark on the side of my left shoulder as it tore my coat and scraped the flesh open as it bolted by. It was a stinging wound, but was not enough to be bothered with at the moment. My total concentration was to keep loading and firing as quickly as possible. The fight was short and upon our charge the enemy started to fall back, but we kept up the pursuit with Colonel Brooke shouting, "Attack! Attack! Keep going boys!" and we did until about 8:00 pm when due to dusk we no longer could see the enemy to push further.

We set up a strong line of skirmishers and pickets surrounding our men and settled in to take care of the wounded and remove the dead. Many of the wounded had burns from the intense heat of the fires and many of the now dead had suffocated from the smoke. It was a terrible sight and I found Buckwheat, who looked as though he was about to fall from exhaustion. I knew from his expression that he no longer considered this to be a game, but he never mentioned a word. I worked my way back to the surgeon's tent for attention to my wound and it was about this time that Franklin Higbe came forward from his position in the rear and told us of the despicable acts he saw from the new recruits.

"Boys, you aren't going to believe what I saw during this push we're doing."

"What was it you witnessed, Franklin?" I asked as I poured some water from my canteen to wash the black powder off my face.

"These new drafters may as well take their damn heels and head back to where they came from. I was back trying to help the artillery boys bring up the cannonade and all of a sudden I looked up and there were five men from our own regiment walking toward me to go the rear. There were two boys under the arms of a wounded man, there were two more following, one had the wounded man's hat and the other had his musket. I looked at the wound on the man and he had a flesh wound on his leg. I couldn't believe it, four men to help a man with a flesh wound. I got so mad I grabbed a musket and held it right up to their faces. I said, 'Boys, there ain't no way that four of you are needed to take this man to the rear. Three of you are going back and get in this fight or you'll be a going to your maker by way of me and my Springfield.' "They stopped, looked at me, looked at my arm, and didn't say a word. They put the hat on the wounded man, gave his musket to one man helping him and the other three just turned and started back to the front. Do you believe this is the kind of new men we have? They are like a bunch of babes who are in need of a suckling mother."

Albert spoke up. "Franklin, these new boys ain't had no training like us. They were pretty much put in a uniform and sent here. You did the right thing, for they should fear us more than they fear the enemy or else we don't have much of chance on winning this war."

That night we settled in to catch a little sleep, but at 3:00 am, we were called up and we knew we were going to start the action up all over again. During the night, General Hancock had brought up the artillery and positioned them to continue the advance against Hill's troops. The fight started back up around 5:00 am and our brigade was held in reserve. Around 9:00 am, we received word from General Hancock to immediately march to our left about two miles to Todd's Tavern as it was reported that Longstreet's Army was moving down the Brock Road in support of Hill's troops and would probably attack our left flank. We marched double quick down the Plank Road until we reached the tavern and immediately began setting up breastworks. Enemy skirmishers were already happening and engaging our men while we worked. Our brigade had little chance of holding off Longstreet if he decided to attack us with great strength; however, it was our luck too that he placed most of his Army in support of A. P. Hill's force and proceeded to counterattack, leaving us to fight it out against a smaller force. We held out until about noon; that's when the men to our right who had been fighting since 5:00 that morning began running out of ammunition and endurance. Hill, being reinforced by Longstreet was now driving our men back and we had to go too. It was just like the battle of Fair Oaks; we had them on the run and now we were the ones in retreat and we had to move fast. Disorder set in and it wasn't until we returned to the safety of our reserve line located at the original point of where we started two days earlier that we were able to stop and reorganize. Once we were there we could make a stand behind the breastworks we'd built. About 4:15pm, the rebels made a final charge to break our lines, but failed after only about one hour of fighting and thus here we lay at the same place as we started, but with around 12,000 less men.

It wasn't long until we received an order from General Grant to once again move the Army towards a place call Spotsylvania. His orders were specific: it was to be a night march so that our Army could arrive before the enemy and take control of the several railroad lines that rested there. If we arrived first, we could capture the supply lines from Hanover Junction, placing the Union Army between Richmond and Lee's Army. This then would force Lee into an open battle or retreat. Even though our losses since we started this campaign were over 20,000 men, Grant was determined not to retreat; his only thoughts were to execute the original plan. The only route we had to Spotsylvania was down the Brock Road, which was nothing more than a wagon road—barely passable. General Meade ordered General Warren to take his Corp down the Brock Road first; our 2nd Corp was to stay in place where the last Confederate attack was while the remaining Army passed by us en-route to Spotsylvania. Our men in the 2nd Corp were totally exhausted and the constant noise of the passing regiments, the smell of smoldering wood and the odor of burned bodies gave us little reprieve to get any rest.

The Brock Road was in such a terrible condition that the Army was moving at a snail's pace. To add more of a dilemma, General Sheridan's cavalry had engaged J.E.B. Stuart's men earlier in the day and had bivouacked along the same road near to Spotsylvania. This stopped the Army's march and General Meade and General Sheridan went into a fiery confrontation as to who was at fault. When Warren's spent soldiers came to a halt, they fell down and slept. It took hours to get them back up in marching order, which caused us to lose the race to Spotsylvania. Lee, anticipating Grant's move to out-flank his Army, moved

General Heath's division as rapidly as feasibly possible to Spotsylvania Court House during the same night. Heath was waiting for Warren's men when they arrived the next morning and the battle of Spotsylvania began.

It is now May 10th and Warren's Corp immediately begins to attack Heath's line upon arrival. As the remaining forces of the two armies arrive on the field, lines are formed on both sides. Our 2nd Corp arrived around 5:00 in the afternoon and we were ordered to take a position in reserve near the Block House Bridge on Warren's left as Warren's Corp was fighting it out with a direct assault on Anderson's middle. After about three hours, General Grant ordered the assault halted and he began prodding the Confederate line looking for a weakness. The Confederate line was strong and straight with trenches and deep traverses defending both flanks. The only flaw in their defense was a half mile arc out from the straight line that consisted of deep trenches; we called this part of their line the "Mule Shoe" as it looked like an inverted "V." Grant ordered General Wright, who took over command when General Sedgwick was killed in his saddle by a sniper, to attack this part of the line to test the defenses while the other Corp was doing the same on the flanks. This task was given to Colonel Upton of the 121st New York. He proposed a new tactic in the attack: he would take 5,000 men or three regiments to the woods edge, some 200 yards from the point of the salient. They would mass together in four lines, shoulder to shoulder. The first regiment would start out at a charge at the point of the inverted "V" and not fire until they reach the trench line. Upon overtaking the enemy's line, this division would turn left and attack the left side of the angle. The second division would follow and turn right and attack the right side of the angle, while the third division would continue the attack going forward.

The attack started at 6 o'clock and within minutes Upton's men had breached the salient's defenses and crushed the Georgian's there. Had he been supported by General Mott's brigade, he would not have had to give back the ground he gained, but darkness came and Colonel Upton had to retreat back to his original line. General Grant was so impressed with this new tactic that he declared, "If three regiments can do this, tomorrow we will try an entire Corp." And that attack would fall squarely on the shoulders of General Hancock and our 2nd Corp.

The next day was May 11th and the day was silent of major fighting. Our officers spent the day with General Grant and General Hancock planning and receiving instructions on what their duty would be and when the attack would begin. All we knew was there was going to be a big fight and it wasn't far off. General Lee, on the other hand, recognized the day off from fighting as Grant's preparations to follow the ambulances and return back across the river towards Fredericksburg as we had done so many times before after major battles. This time he was planning to attack our retreating forces in the hopes of ending the war in pursuit. This miscalculation caused General Lee to start dismantling some of the cannon protecting the salient in preparation to move out in pursuit. At midnight, we were ordered to rise and prepare to do battle. Franklin Jones, Albert Marsh, young Buckwheat and I managed to keep ourselves in a tight pack as we began to maneuver towards the point of attack directly in front of the salient. Albert and Franklin told me that if we were lucky enough to make it to the inside of the Mule Shoe without getting killed, they were going to move to capture the regimental flags. If we could secure them from the enemy early, the rest would surrender. Earlier in the evening it had started to rain and now it was a torrential downpour combined with a thick fog making it difficult to slog through the deep woods. This massive amount of constant rain along with the fog helped to keep our movement towards the southern picket lines quiet.

It as now about 4:00 am; the rain was a good distraction, for it takes our minds off the deed we are about to undertake. Buckwheat is sticking pretty close to the three of us; it was as if we have come to adopt his character into our inner circle or what is left of it. We are now approaching the edge of the woods and there remains an open field of about 200 yards for us to cross without firing a shot. The fog and rain is still our friend, but keeping the powder dry may become difficult once the action begins. We waited in silence until all our lines were formed, and then around 4:30 am we heard the order: "Fix bayonets and move forward at the double quick!"

It wasn't more than 30 seconds later we heard officers yelling, "Charge!" at the loudest of voices and with that we all let out yells that could have been heard all the way to Washington. We ran as fast as our legs could go and as we approached the breastworks the orders came to "Fire at will!" and a volley of balls was let loose that killed many a man. Our first line felt the sting of the enemy sentries and they fell to the ground quickly, but with so many of us heading to the same point we soon began to pour over their breastworks. Hand to hand fighting began as reloading was now quite impossible. Our line had orders to turn to the right once inside the Mule Shoe and this we did. Albert and Franklin were moving quickly to the colors with Buckwheat and I close behind. We ran into a bunch of Rebs who had grabbed their muskets and were trying to stop our advance. Albert kept moving, ignoring the Rebs, but the rest of us had to spear our way through. Cannons were now responding from the enemy's back lines and grape was falling around all combatants. As we continued to fight, a Reb stuck me from behind in the shoulder and the pain was searing. I went down, but before he could finish me off, Buckwheat stuck him in the gut. I was able to rise, but felt confused and that's when I saw Albert. He had captured the flags of the 44th Virginia Regiment once so proud to be a part of Stonewall Jackson's Brigade. Shouts went up all around as Albert started waving the flag with his blue uniform in control. Our boys were coming in now faster than ever; the Rebs were throwing up their arms by the hundreds and then I heard a loud cannon ball drop near by and when the smoke cleared, Albert was down, but still holding on to the enemy's colors. Buckwheat ran over to

Albert, whose right leg was a mess. Franklin was down also; he had taken a bayonet in his side. By now, our support from General Wright's Corp were coming in and pushing the Rebels back even further. Some boys came up from our reserve and started helping all of us get back behind the lines. Cheers were all around Albert throughout as he still held on to the captured colors as they carried him off the field.

Buckwheat said, "James, you'll be alright, these boys will take you back. I've got to keep going; I will check on you when we are done here."

"Take care—act fast and don't delay your effort," I told him and began walking back. Blood was coming out of my shoulder pretty quick now, and I was beginning to feel light headed.

I must have passed out somewhere while trying to get behind our lines. When I awoke it was daylight and still raining, and I found myself lying on the ground near a surgeon's tent. Someone had plugged my wound to slow the blood loss, but I found I couldn't move my arm even though it was still attached, which I was happy about. I tried to rise and that's when a soldier came over and helped me up.

"We need to get you further back; the Rebs have brought up reinforcements and are counter-attacking now," he said.

Once on my feet, I was able to walk while holding onto this soldier's arm. I still felt light headed, but was able to keep pace and fortunately made it to the ambulance wagons whereupon I completely collapsed and passed out again. The next time I awoke I found myself lying in a tent with other wounded soldiers. I looked around and once again I found the horrors of war surrounding me. A hospital nurse came in to the tent and noticing my alertness.

"It's good you awoke; you've been out for two days now. You didn't lose your arm, but it was close. You will take some time to heal."

I couldn't find any words to speak with. I was still trying to establish myself. Finally, I said to the nurse, "Where am I?"

"You are near Fredericksburg," he said, "and will remain here for a few more days until there is enough room to send you to a hospital in Washington." With that he handed me a small amount of opium to drink saying, "Take this, it will help with the pain." It wasn't long after my swallow that I fell back off into a sleep.

I awoke some hours later still lying in the same spot. This time the nurse asked me if I felt hungry and I replied that I could use some substance. I sat up and looked as best I could at my injury. The bandages were wrapped around my neck and under my arm and also around my breast. The pain was great when I moved rapidly, but bearable. When the nurse returned I ask him how the battle was going.

"I believe this one is over. We were doing really well at the Mule Shoe in the beginning, but then the Confederates counter-attacked. One General named

Samuel McGowan destroyed our Michigan regiment with his South Carolinians in a hand to hand struggle. That defeat started our men to retreat back to the original line we had captured earlier."

I sat there listening to him describe the battle and found myself thinking about Albert and Franklin, both carrying severe injuries. I wondered where they may be and how they are, but there were about 20,000 men either dead or wounded and to find them would be like looking for a needle in a haystack. I started to feel depressed as none of us in the inner circle of eight who started out from Randolph were able to continue the fight any longer. Franklin Higbe was the only one able to carry on some sort of duty, even though he had only one arm.

I remained here in this hospital camp for another three days and then we received word that the Army was moving again towards Richmond to a place called Hanover Junction. The hospital also had to move, but the men here with me were to go to Washington as soon as transportation could be obtained.

As all of us who were injured arrived at the Convalescent Home in Washington, I remember my previous visit which was among some of my unhappiest memories of the past few years. Once established, I was at last able to obtain some paper, so I immediately sat down to write letters back home. At least my injury was on the opposite side of my writing hand and I was able to inform everyone where I was and what my condition was. However, my letter to Emma was more detailed. I explained to her that I believed I would no longer be able to return to our company as my injury would take longer to heal than my remaining enlistment time left and if she was still willing, we should set a time to marry when I arrived back home. Part of me was happy to be injured and be guaranteed to return to my Emma; the other part of me was sad to not be able to continue the fight. I sent off the letters and began the slow process of healing.

The time was now is July and I am able to walk without any assistance, but I still cannot move my arm because of severe pain, but at least my fingers are starting to move upon the command of my mind. Our Army has continued to move ever closer to Richmond with no signs of retreat. They have fault battles at Hanover Court House and Cold Harbor and now are presenting the terror of our siege to Petersburg. But the word from the front is telling us of deep, long trenches being dug by both sides with a constant bombardment of artillery on either side, but no major assaults. It was as if men on both sides were no longer willing to risk what remained of their armies on an offensive maneuver. I suspected that Grant was using his head and allowing the supply lines of food, men and supplies to be cut off by Sheridan and Burnside while he was sitting in front of Lee's main Army defending Richmond.

I have received letters from home from many members of my family as well as from my beloved Emma. She is making plans for our wedding in a few months and it lifts my spirit every time I read her words. I have sent a letter to Buckwheat and Franklin Higbe to learn of our regiment's condition, but have not had a response yet.

In late July I received a letter from Franklin Higbe, informing me that the Division was camp outside Petersburg and all the fighting seems to be just firing from one trench to another trench. Grant's focus is to starve the Rebels out and to keep bombarding them into submission. Sherman has continued his march to cut the south in half and is camped just outside Atlanta, bombarding Johnson's forces there too. He also informed me that our raw recruit, Buckwheat had been killed at Cold Harbor. He said he died as well as any veteran fighter. He was a quick learner, but he took big chances and lost his luck one day. Franklin Jones has returned to service and they have made him a Lieutenant. Albert Marsh has been awarded the Medal of Honor for his bravery at Spotsylvania and the medal will be presented to him by the President as soon as he has healed enough. With his demeanor it may be difficult for him to get around on just one leg without issuing a few swear words for comfort, but he is of strong character and will prevail. He was also named soldier of the month for our regiment and has received a $100 reward.

After reading Franklin's letter, I stopped to wonder about the eight of us who sat together on the train to Elmira almost three years earlier. Six of us are out of the war, Franklin Higbe is no longer able to fight, but his spirit prevails. The only one left in action is Franklin Jones. He started as a plain, unassuming man actuated by honorable motives, sincere in his dealings and his conviction to the Almighty. He is a strong friend and an upright individual, a just man who carries the respect and friendship of all classes. I am sure he is destined to survive this war.

It is early August and I am able to move my fingers and bend my arm without being distraught from pain. I have been released to do fatigue duty and have been assigned to a paper processing position, which I must say is one of the most terrible jobs in the Army. But I only have about 30 days and my enlistment will be over and then I can return home to my Emma.

On August 14th I received a letter from Ma, which was to be one of the most painful letters I have ever read, as it destroyed my human soul as I read each word. It started out: "Son, it is with great pain and agony that I must write to you with such sorrowful news. I must inform you that your beloved Emma has passed on to the hereafter. God has decided he needed her beside him and he took her instantly. Emma was on her way to the convalescent home as usual and had stopped at a railroad crossing, but when the train whistle blew, her horse reared suddenly and bolted crossing the track with such force that the carriage overturned and fell upon her body. I know the loss is great for you and for those of us here at home as well. We will always remember her as being tender and forceful, unassuming and yet full of courage and resources; she gave of herself without stint to the service and happiness of others. She always exerted a strong influence for truth and good natured living. Her gracious memory will never depart from the hearts who knew her, I am so sorry to have to be the one to inform you in such a manner but prolonging the report would do no good, your Mother."

I laid the letter down and stared into the wall. How could this have happened to my beloved Emma? I felt as if someone had just torn my heart from my chest. I became angry and bitter as I blamed the war for the loss of my beloved, for if it wasn't for this war she would not have been venturing to a convalescent home to help the wounded. I would not be sitting here trying to heal my wounds and the constant agony in my mind of all the tragedies I have seen in the last three years. What started out as an adventure to see the rest of our country has turned into a trip to the Devil's Den itself.

As the rest of August expired, I began to prepare for my departure from this Army. I no longer wrote to anyone, my mind was still full of bitterness of the human atrocities I have seen and experienced, I could not get my dear Emma's face out of my mind. I no longer speak to anyone and only respond partially when called upon. I am tired of the sight of all people, for among them I only see the face of death waiting in the wings of life to pounce upon each of them at a moment's notice. I arranged for my final ticket home from Washington and upon my discharge I took my seat for the final trip in a soldier's uniform. I have made a decision to see my family one last time and then to leave Randolph for good—never to return—for the pain I carry in my chest is too hard to render on a daily basis. I have decided to go to a place where there is but a few people and no war. I have heard of the great Rocky Mountains, abundant in wild game and a person may go months without seeing another human being. This will be the place I am destined to go; to be alone as that is all my soul demands at this point.

For five years now, I have lived in or around the isolation of the Rocky Mountains. I have become accustomed to life without the aid of another human being. However, I recently have allowed my mind to wonder of the men with whom I lived and fought with for three years and of their consequence following the war, so I wrote a letter to Lemuel and he responded in kind to me with an accounting of each of our friends. Albert Marsh returned to Randolph and was made Postmaster by the President. He has now become a grocer and is living with his sister in Randolph. Franklin Higbe returned to Randolph in November of 1864. He moved his wife and children to Friendship, Wisconsin, to live on his brother's farm. Franklin Jones went on to become a captain in our regiment. He was at Appomattox when Lee surrendered, and returned home to become a County Sheriff. As for Lemuel, he returned home after his stint at hard labor and fathered four more children. He continued his surveying and farmed when there was no work.

As for me, I continue to roam this vast land, hunting, trapping, and doing a little mining. The past memories are slowly leaving my skull; I no longer see death upon every person I come in contact with and the silence has allowed me to sort through my past, but the haunting loss of my Emma seems to be beyond repair. Perhaps someday, I will once again become a man without pain. Only God knows.

2135085

Made in the USA